NARCOTICS AND CRIME CONTROL

NARCOTICS AND CRIME CONTROL

By

MICHAEL D. LYMAN, B.S., M.S.
University of Missouri-Columbia
Law Enforcement Training Institute
School of Law

With a Foreword by

Samuel G. Chapman
Professor, University of Oklahoma
Norman, Oklahoma

CHARLES C THOMAS • PUBLISHER
Springfield • Illinois • U.S.A.

Published and Distributed Throughout the World by

CHARLES C THOMAS • PUBLISHER
2600 South First Street
Springfield, Illinois 62794-9265

ISBN 0-398-05347-2

Library of Congress Catalog Card Number: 87-6505

With THOMAS BOOKS *careful attention is given to all details of manufacturing and design. It is the Publisher's desire to present books that are satisfactory as to their physical qualities and artistic possibilities and appropriate for their particular use.* THOMAS BOOKS *will be true to those laws of quality that assure a good name and good will.*

Printed in the United States of America
Q-R-3

Library of Congress Cataloging in Publication Data

Lyman, Michael D.
Narcotics and crime control.

Bibliography: p.
Includes index.
1. Drug abuse--United States. 2. Narcotics, Control of--United States. 3. Narcotics dealers--United States. 4. Narcotic enforcement agents--United States. 5. Drug abuse--United States--Prevention. 6. Narcotics and crime--United States. I. Title.
HV5825.L96 1987 363.4'5'0973 87-6505
ISBN 0-398-05347-2

FOREWORD

THE LITERATURE of narcotics and crime control is extensive and expanding in near quantum fashion ever since the senseless, highly publicized drug-related deaths of John Belushi, Len Bias and Don Rogers, American figures prominent in entertainment and professional athletics. When one reviews the literature, writings prepared by attorneys, legislators, physicians, sociologists, psychiatrists, coaches, addicts, corporate tycoons, athletic franchise owners, psychologists, students, parents, social workers, former hippies and gang members and an endless array of others are found. Everyone writes as an expert, professing to present inside information. Common to the writings is the fact that not many people understand the totality of the drug scene and its massive societal implications. Consequently, the field begs for a suitably descriptive reference book, something which one does not find in today's literature.

Professor Lyman's book, *Narcotics and Crime Control,* fills this immense void and does so in terms that lay people can readily understand. Well written, it spares the reader from the long words, technical terms, academic jargon and endless statistics and legalese about what needs to be done to get drug enforcement and control back on the track.

Refreshingly, the book is well organized. Comprised of four parts, the reader is first introduced to the world of drugs. Here, Professor Lyman presents a historical look at drug use, familiarizes his readership with classes of drugs, and identifies the source nations. He forthrightly talks about how profit is made by those who deal drugs illicitly, noting that money is what attracts many people and organizations to become involved in the first place and to stay involved even while ruining other peoples' lives.

Having set this stage, Professor Lyman introduces the players: manufacturers, traffickers, distributors, dealers, users and agents, among others. He also talks about informers and their motives as well as the extent to which and how organized crime interests are intermingled with the drug world. Sections on how motorcycle gangs and gangs in prison feature drugs are especially revealing.

The third part is on drug enforcement. In it, Professor Lyman writes about drug laws, which he colorfully calls the "narc's tool box." He also writes revealingly about drug investigations, inter-agency cooperation and coordination, investigative techniques and the kind of equipment agents have at their disposal, roles in investigations, and how people smuggle drugs. The relationship between drugs and crime is explored, too.

Narcotics and Crime Control concludes with a discussion of drugs on the job, drug testing, and treatment and prevention programs. These issues are not just timely and relevant to understanding the drug problem and what can be done about it, they are *urgent* considerations.

The book is a comprehensive sourcebook which provides reliable information about the illicit business of drugs, drug trafficking and enforcement practices. It is an honest, no-nonsense book which addresses issues in a business where factual and reliable information has been difficult to find. The content of *Narcotics and Crime Control* has been meticulously culled from a vast array of information which has, in bits and pieces, been presented through technical papers, staff reports and memoranda, news magazines, newspapers, technical journals, police reports, intelligence documents, and reports from the U.S. Bureau of Justice Statistics, the U.S. Department of Justice, the U.S. Drug Enforcement Administration, the National Institute of Drug Abuse, the President's Commission on organized crime, and from policies of various enforcement agencies.

Why should Professor Lyman write this book and what qualifies him to do so? It is done because the book is needed and Lyman has the education, professional background and the ability and determination to put it together. During his twelve years of professional life, Professor Lyman has served as a senior agent, criminal investigator, trainer and teacher and as the public information officer for the Oklahoma State Bureau of Narcotics and Dangerous Drugs. His early experience was as a special agent with the Kansas Bureau of Investigation. He earned his undergraduate and graduate degrees the hard way from Wichita State University, doing so while working drug cases for the KBI. He knows the narcotics scene, the actors, the court processes, the prisons' world, the games narcs play, the equipment, the pressures, the debilitating family life, and so forth, firsthand. He writes with perceptive understanding.

In conclusion, the most potent weapon against narcotics is intelligent prevention. In order to prevent something, the issue must first be understood. *Narcotics and Crime Control* is important to helping people understand the complexities of this monolith, its scale and scope, and the strategies which may be taken to get at the drug menace. This is a book of unusual worth which deserves acclaim as a significant contribution to the literature. May it be widely circulated and read!

Samuel G. Chapman
University of Oklahoma

PREFACE

IN THE LATE 1960s and early 1970s, I was living as a college student in a major university city. The drug menace then was gaining considerable momentum and coincided with much of the unrest of that era. In spite of campus riots, demonstrations, and a general anti-establishment atmosphere, I personally abstained from illicit drug use, even though I observed much of it happening around me. I not only considered drug consumption as trendy, I rejected it on the basis of its illegality.

In 1974, I accepted employment as a narcotics agent in order to enhance my credentials for a regular position with a police department. My first year required me to learn the needed skills "on the job."

I soon had occasion to purchase a small quantity of heroin from a fifteen-year-old kid at a suburban Kansas City video arcade. This was by no means considered a major case, but after a few heroin transactions I was able to meet the kid's drug connection. I was surprised to learn that the source was a forty-seven-year-old man who had been using the kid to sell heroin for over a year. I was also surprised to learn that the supplier was, in fact, the kid's own father.

This case demonstrated a dimension to the job which I did not fully understand but found intriguing. My interest in the illicit drug business was subsequently captivated, and I later chose to pursue a career in drug enforcement. During the next ten years, I worked for two state law enforcement agencies: the Kansas Bureau of Investigation and the Oklahoma Bureau of Narcotics and Dangerous Drugs.

Working undercover for these organizations provided me opportunities to work street-level drug crimes and meet high-level organized crime figures in both rural areas and big cities.

Probably the most significant lesson learned while working the streets is that the educational process is continuous and one can never learn too much when dealing with criminals. Every drug buy is routine yet unpredictable, every drug raid is a life-and-death situation, and assumptions are frequently laced with doubts. It is difficult to become too comfortable with any particular drug enforcement strategy, because things always change.

Many qualified sources were called on to assist in the preparation of this text and should rightfully be acknowledged. Striving for a text representative of many different drug enforcement situations, I culled information from drug enforcement agencies in five states who I had worked with, including: Oklahoma, Kansas, Arkansas, Texas, and Missouri.

In particular, those who made specific contributions to this work were Director Tom Heggy and Narcotics Agents David Dagg and James Dempewolf of the Oklahoma Bureau of Narcotics and Dangerous Drugs Control; Special Agent David Christy of the Kansas Bureau of Investigation for expertise and advice; Lieutenant David Davis, Dallas Police Department, for providing technical advice; Detective Mike Himmel of the Columbia Police Department for advice and expertise; Attorney Joe Moseley, Boone County Prosecutor, who provided technical legal advice for portions of the text; Sheriff Lawrence Riffenburg, Laclede County, Missouri, for providing photos; Doctor Tom Buckles, Director of Criminal Justice, Columbia College, for technical expertise and support; Earnest Sjoblom, of the Missouri Bureau of Narcotics and Dangerous Drugs, for technical expertise and charts; U.S. Marshal Lee Koury, U.S. Marshal's Service, for providing photos; Sergeant Rod Combs, of the Arkansas State Police, for technical advice and photos; Attorney Keith Lyman, for legal counseling and moral support; and Director Wayne Thomason and the staff of the Law Enforcement Training Institute, for patience, encouragement, and understanding throughout this project.

Special recognition is deserved by Rita M. Walther, of the University of Missouri-Columbia, Conferences and Short Courses Department, who provided the artwork and illustrations for this text; Marty Patton of the University of Missouri-Columbia, English Department, for diligent editorial services, professional support, and considerate perseverance; and Darlene Ward for tireless moral support and nerves of iron.

In addition, this text serves as a tribute to those dedicated drug enforcement officers, past and present, who have chosen one of the most dangerous, frustrating and yet important jobs in law enforcement, a job whose very existence poses a paramount threat to every facet of the illicit drug trafficking underground.

M. D. L.

INTRODUCTION

FOR CENTURIES man has demonstrated a fascination with substances that alter his consciousness and state of mind. This age-old curiosity continues to intrigue many phases of today's otherwise modern and intelligent society. The simple ancient practice of self-intoxication has evolved throughout history into one of the most costly and tragic international disasters ever.

With modern-day transportation and communications, the entrepreneurs of today's drug culture have managed to establish a stronghold in every level of society throughout the world. Allured by massive profits that can be acquired quickly and easily, these criminals have evolved to accept cold-blooded violence and an array of criminal activities as everyday business considerations.

Although drug consumption has long since been a problem for society, the popularity of drugs in the turbulent 1960s created a demand for illicit substances that is still growing twenty years later, in spite of massive public awareness campaigns.

Combating the problem is an ever-pressing issue in political campaigns, public interest surveys, treatment philosophies, and law enforcement priorities. The problem, however, has not seen much of a downturn in spite of suppression efforts by all concerned.

With all of the publications and media coverage seen everyday, it is still surprising how many members of the educational and law enforcement communities as well as the general public fail to understand the origin and magnitude of the problem or what is currently being done about it.

The problem of domestic drug production, for example, has drastically increased the influx of marijuana, PCP, methamphetamine, and designer drugs on American streets. This is creating, in some instances, a lower street price for the drugs due to their greater availability. Unfortunately, the lower the prices, the more affordable the drug is and the greater the demand for it. This activity has also created a more dangerous type of criminal whose technology in guerrilla-type anti-police tactics has posed a new threat to drug enforcement agents.

Furthermore, with the concentration of federal task forces on our coastal cities, international drug smugglers are seeking other ports of entry and methods for introducing their contraband into the United States. This has created an increase in air and ground smuggling activity for more inland areas of the country.

Recent awareness of drug consumption on the job has only served to compound the already perplexing substance abuse dilemma.

With new research showing the increasing dangers of drug use, drug trafficking, financial responsibility, employer liability, and accidents causing disability and death, more people are beginning to understand the far-reaching implications of an illegal business which still remains, for the most part, misunderstood.

The minor drug problem of the 1940s has certainly festered over the years to what we read about on almost a daily basis in the local newspapers. With newfound dangers on almost a weekly basis, it is difficult to understand how our society has acquired such a tolerance for such a tragically widespread epidemic of shattered lives and death. Perhaps the answer lies in realizing that the "hippies" and radical factions of yesterday's society are, in fact, today's parents, judges, prosecutors, and even policemen, and may be major contributors to the country's current drug posture.

This text is designed to provide answers to many of the most commonly asked questions regarding drugs, those who deal them, and those who have chosen to fight the war against them.

M. D. L.

CONTENTS

NARCOTICS AND CRIME CONTROL

Part I

A WORLD OF DRUGS

THERE IS nothing new about drug abuse. People from all corners of the world have rationalized the effects of substance abuse for thousands of years and continue to do so throughout our society.

When attempting to understand the big picture of drug use and the drug-trafficking business, it is logical to survey the history of illicit as well as legal drug consumption and identify those drugs that are considered to pose the greatest problems to society today. Additionally, it is important to identify the origin of these illicit substances and those countries that are most instrumental in their manufacture and distribution.

CHAPTER 1

THE DRUG LEGACY

IT MIGHT BE surprising for some people today to realize that drug use in the past parallels, in many respects, drug use today. As we examine the history of global drug abuse, we will further see how the traditional consumption of illicit substances seems to continue in spite of the disease, addiction, crime, and emotional pain experienced by drug users and their loved ones. Especially surprising is the current drug consumption rate in light of our country's extensive drug abuse history, as well as current anti-drug and public awareness campaigns by concerned government agencies and private interest groups.

It is not logical to assume that the problem will just go away on its own or that hard-line drug enforcement policies are solely an adequate solution. Perhaps, as an enlightened society with more collective resources at our disposal than ever before, we can study mistakes previously made and create a workable solution to this deadly menace.

JUSTIFICATIONS FOR DRUG CONSUMPTION

To better understand our current drug abuse status, perhaps we should first examine the reasons why users choose to involve themselves with substance abuse in the first place. It is certainly no secret that people, for generations and generations, have had a desire to alter their senses for any number of reasons. Some reasons for drug consumption are recreational use such as social drinking, while other reasons are practical, such as the administration of drugs for medical treatment. Some of the justifications for drug use will be discussed next.

One of the original uses of mind-altering drugs was to enhance **religious ceremonies** in an effort to become closer to God or nature.

Natives of ancient India, as well as the Aztecs of Mexico, relied heavily on the effects of organic hallucinogenic drugs that were derived from shrubs and plants.

The traditional use of drugs to aid in the **treatment of disease** has been commonplace throughout history. When drugs such as morphine and opium were used extensively as painkillers and local anesthetics, the addictive side effects were merely considered secondary. Marijuana prepared as a medicinal herbal tea was popular in ancient India as far back as 2001 B.C., and it is likely these people were the first to have smoked it for its recreational effects.

Social interaction has always played a major role in traditional as well as current drug use trends. The natives of Peru and Bolivia have chewed the coca leaf for generations for both its medicinal and recreational effects.

In the seventeenth and eighteenth centuries, the Chinese popularized opium dens as a sanctuary for the smoking of opium or "chasing the dragon." A modern-day equivalent of the opium den might be the bar scene, where cocaine, marijuana, and designer drugs are commonly consumed as well as alcohol.

History has shown us that many people involved in the arts, especially music and literature, have felt that altering of their moods through drug consumption helped to **enhance creativity** and inspiration. For example, the famous American writer Edgar Allen Poe was partial to tincture of opium while many of Sigmund Freud's earlier writings were inspired by regular use of cocaine.

Many people attempt to relieve anxiety or boredom by **altering** their **moods** through drug consumption. In the late 1950s the use of Valium and Librium by housewives became almost commonplace. In fact, a significant percentage of the pharmaceutical drugs prescribed by physicians today are for mood-altering purposes.

The final reason, and possibly the saddest, is old-fashioned **peer pressure.** This powerful force penetrates all stratas of society with regard to the clothes we wear, the cars we drive, and how we conduct ourselves socially. It is common for those not interested in drug use to be persuaded by their peers to indulge in drug consumption to avoid being considered "un-cool" or an outcast in the group. This occurs with all age groups of children as well as adults and is considered a major factor of drug use in the 1980s.

THE HISTORY

The drug legacy began thousands of years ago in areas such as India, China, and Central America, where cannabis, ephedra, and opium were considered to be good health remedies. The medicinal use of these plants turned to recreational use, creating a pattern of use to abuse that has continued to the present. This pattern, thousands of years old, accounts for generations of human suffering.

It was in the early 1700s when **caffeine,** discovered as an extract from the Ethiopian coffee tree, first came to Europe. During this same period of history **coca** from South America, **tobacco** from Central America, and **hallucinogens** from North America were also becoming popular. During that time, there were many recreational, religious, and medical uses for these drugs and they were graciously received by European courts, along with other popular commodities such as parrots, furs, and gold.

Europeans, in 1545, first introduced Americans to alcohol and to **cannabis,** which was imported from Asia. Alcoholic beverages generally have been accepted throughout history as a popular element in social gatherings. Cannabis, while originally used as hemp for the manufacturing of rope, would later be grown in large acreages by hundreds of farmers across the country.

The popular use of tobacco as a recreational pastime spread almost globally in the 1650s. While its use was taking hold, the use of **opium** in various forms was spreading throughout Europe and China.

By the late 1770s, the smoking of opium in China had gotten so far out of hand that Chinese rulers made it a capital offense. Importing of opium into China was finally prohibited in 1839 by the Manchu government. This national ban was aimed primarily at the English, who were the main suppliers of the drug. Consequently, war broke out between the English and Chinese over this sensitive trade issue and thus emerged the first known war over drugs, later referred to as the "Opium War," which lasted from 1839 to 1842. Ultimately, China was defeated by England who vowed to defend its global trade prerogatives. The English even justified their involvement in the war by encouraging the importation of opium to their own shores.

Opium did, in fact, become a major health concern in the eighteenth and nineteenth century in Europe, primarily due to strong concentrations of the drug in many common British medicines. Toward the end of the nineteenth century, opium use was considered to be an epidemic in both England and America. In fact, much of the abuse was attributed to the use of children's medications which had such names as: Munn's Elixir, Godfrey's Cordial, and Mother Bailey's Quieting Syrup. Finally, in 1803, a "cure" was discovered for opium addiction. This new substance, **morphine,** was a derivative of the opium poppy and was not originally considered to be addictive, since it was injected into the bloodstream rather than digested through the stomach.

The following drugs were also identified during this general period of history:

Ether—Discovered in 1730
Nitrous Oxide (laughing gas)—Discovered in 1776
Chloroform—Discovered in 1831
Chloral Hydrate (Mickey Finn)—Discovered in 1869
Mescaline (the hallucinogenic property in Peyote)—Discovered in 1896

With the outbreak of the American Civil War in the 1860s, most battlefield surgery was conducted with morphine as a local painkiller. Administered with the use of the newly discovered hypodermic needle, much of the necessary **use** of morphine spread to **abuse,** resulting in an estimated 400,000 addicts in the army alone. After the war was over, the country experienced a vast national drug reliance on morphine, due primarily to self-treatment, and was later termed the "soldier's disease."

Many opiate-based medicines were then marketed in the United States under harmless-sounding names like Ayer's Cherry Pectoral, Hooper's Anodyne, the Infant's Friend, and Mrs. Winslow's Soothing Syrup.

The late 1860s also saw the migration of thousands of Chinese to California to work on the railroads, and with the Chinese came their addictions to opium and their underground opium dens. These migrant workers would work on the railroads and then return to their homes in coastal cities of California, where opium dens grew in numbers. A significant Chinese population was established in San Francisco by 1875, which was also the year of the first recorded anti-drug law in the United States. This law was a San Francisco city ordinance that prohibited opium smoking in the city limits, but it proved difficult to enforce and provided little deterrence for drug abuse.

During the following sixty years, twenty-seven other cities passed similar laws. Finally, in 1909, the United States government bowed to public pressure and passed legislation against opium, making it a federal criminal offense.

Cocaine appeared on the national drug scene in 1878 and was thought to be a wonder drug for many ailments, as well as a common local anesthetic and cure for morphine addiction. While the alleged benefits of cocaine were spreading during the late 1800s, an opiate liver pill merchant named John Pemberton began experimentation with extracts from coca leaves, caffeine from the kola nut, and wine, calling his new creation Coca-Cola®. In 1906, the United States government finally required the coca leaf derivatives to be removed from the beverage.

During this period many new drugs and chemical compounds were discovered. **Heroin,** first thought to be a cure for morphine addiction, was extracted from the opium poppy plant. In 1898, it was commercially manufactured by the Bayer Company in Germany and was considered to be up to three times as potent as morphine. Other significant drugs were rapidly achieving popularity, such as amphetamines (originally synthesized in 1887) and barbiturates in 1903.

As drug consumption escalated, medical experts identified many new health risks. In 1906, the original **Food and Drug Act** was designed to protect the consumer by requiring opium-based drugs to state so on their labels. Another important drug control measure taken during this period of history was the enactment of the **Harrison Narcotic Act** in 1914.

This comprehensive law was considered a major piece of legislation, because it required licensing and taxation of those who dispensed preparations containing coca or opium extracts. Furthermore, it required that only licensed physicians be permitted to write prescriptions for these types of drugs.

This law proved to be a double-edged sword. While it was aimed at curbing the national addiction rate by licensing drug handlers, it failed to define the term "addiction" and subsequently had no provisions for the treatment of those who were already addicted. This forced existing addicts to acquire their drugs elsewhere and, ironically, might have been the original basis for the drug-smuggling underground as we now know it.

The roaring twenties spawned an escalation in the general use of marijuana that continued through the 1930s. Marijuana use was blamed, in part, for the crime wave of the thirties. Public outrage for the drug resulted in propaganda films such as *Reefer Madness,* which depicted marijuana users as becoming criminally insane after smoking the drug.

In 1937, the *Marijuana Tax Act* was enacted by the federal government and outlawed the possession or sale of the drug. Like many drug laws that preceded this one, the deterrent effect was marginal. Interestingly enough, at the time of the passing of this act, over 10,000 acres of marijuana were being cultivated in the United States, with primary production in New York, California, and the southern United States. With the earlier invention of the cotton gin, domestic production of marijuana was drastically decreasing.

The popularity of marijuana continued into the 1950s along with other drug fads such as glue sniffing and the use of Valium and Librium. Toward the end of this decade another drug, claiming mind-altering properties, was emerging. This drug, LSD (lysergic acid diethylamide), was popularized by former Harvard professor, Doctor Timothy Leary.

The turbulent 1960s emerged as a major arena for the promotion of illicit drug use, which saw the popularizing of such drugs as LSD, marijuana, amphetamines, and other newly developed drugs like MDA, STP, and DMA. Escalating drug abuse in the 1960s was one component of an era of unrest involving demonstrations targeted at the war in Vietnam, civil rights, and women's liberation.

The social standards of the baby boom generation carried over into the early 1970s, and by this time public awareness of the dangers of certain drugs was becoming commonplace. It was in 1970 that another major drug law was enacted known as **The Comprehensive Drug Abuse Prevention and Control Act of 1970** (The Controlled Substances Act). This significant drug control act updated all federal drug laws since the Harrison narcotic Act of 1914 and provided for the scheduling of all substances believed to be dangerous (see Chapter 2 on "Drug Familiarization"). Furthermore, the act set forth nine control mechanisms for the distributing, manufacturing, purchasing and general handling of controlled substances by legally registered handlers.

PCP or phencyclidine had achieved significant popularity on the illicit drug scene by the early 1970s and was, at first, thought to be a safe hallucinogenic drug with effects like LSD. Negative publicity about horrible side effects and bad trips soon flooded the drug culture as PCP proved to be one of the most dangerous drugs on the illicit market. Due to the overdose death rate of the drug, President Jimmy Carter enacted emergency legislation against it in 1978.

Posing an equally great threat in the late 1970s and the early 1980s was the widespread recreational use of methaqualone tablets, otherwise known as Quaaludes, or "ludes." Though manufactured legally in the United States until 1981, this was the drug of choice for many abusers and proved to be so dangerous that even its legitimate use was ultimately prohibited.

In the late 1970s a new public threat evolved: clandestine or **underground chemical laboratories.** These laboratories manufactured large amounts of PCP, LSD, and methamphetamine powder, which were becoming more commonplace. The popularity of these drugs has lingered into the 1980s just as the demand for cocaine is increasing. From a relatively obscure drug with moderate public appeal, cocaine has an unbridled popularity with almost all age groups and strata of society.

In 1986, cocaine's widespread popularity gave birth to a new cocaine derivative called **crack,** which is a smokeable or "freebase" form of cocaine. Almost overnight, crack demonstrated the dark side of cocaine to the American drug-using population due to widespread publicity about its deadly negative effects. In addition, this era has witnessed the development of **designer drugs,** which claim to possess all of the "good" effects of controlled drugs but without the negative effects (bad trips) and are supposedly perfectly legal to possess. The claims are, of course, untrue on both counts, as these new drugs have claimed many fatalities since 1985.

Finally, in 1986, Congress passed the most far-reaching drug law ever, the **Anti-Drug Abuse Act** of 1986. This comprehensive drug control act won final approval on October 17, 1986 and increased federal financing for law enforcement, drug treatment, and education programs. In addition, it provided for stiffer penalties in federal drug cases, including life terms for kingpins of major drug-trafficking networks.

The legacy of drug use represents a myriad of events evolving into continuing drug synthesis, changing drug laws, and personal experiences, although the dilemma appears to be here to stay. As an intelligent society, we can only strive to understand the problem to better formulate the solution.

The understanding of cause-and-effect variables of drug use discussed in the upcoming chapters will hopefully contribute to the final solution in controlling the problems associated with illicit substances.

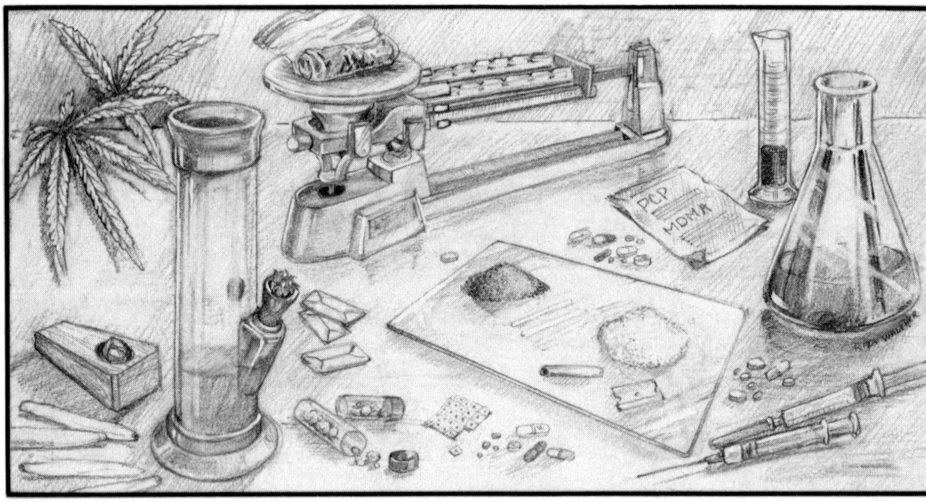
PCP
MDMA

The overall differences in the preceding four categories are defined as follows:

Stimulants

Stimulants are defined as drugs that stimulate the central nervous system and increase the activity of the brain or spinal cord.

Effects: Greater energy
Increased alertness
A feeling of euphoria
Irritability

Widely abused stimulants are anti-obesity drugs, amphetamines, and cocaine. Other widely abused stimulants are nicotine and caffeine, even though they have a lesser effect on the body.

Depressants

Depressant drugs are those drugs that slow down or actually depress the central nervous system, diminishing or stopping vital body functions. Their action is irregular because they do not depress all parts of the central nervous system at once.

The term "depressants" is somewhat misleading, however, because such drugs might actually elevate a person's mood at first. The term has no direct relationship to "depression," except that consistent use of depressants can cause a form of psychological depression.

Effects: Slurred speech
Drunken behavior
Dilated pupils
Disorientation

Hallucinogens

These are defined as drugs that act on the central nervous system and produce mood and perceptual changes varying from sensory illusion to hallucinations. LSD and PCP are examples of synthetic hallucinogens, although drugs such as peyote and mescaline are naturally occurring substances that can also be produced synthetically.

Effects: Psychosis
Poor perception of time and space

Narcotics

Narcotics are defined as drugs which depress the central nervous system with analgesic and sedative properties. Under U.S. laws narcotics are considered to be addictive drugs that produce physical and psychological dependence.

Effects: Euphoria
Drowsiness
Watery eyes
Chills and sweating

THE DRUG SCHEDULES

As we noted earlier, the Controlled Substances Act of 1970 imposed many controls and requirements for drug manufacturers, physicians, and other registrants. One of the main functions of this law was to isolate and label those drugs that were considered to be the most dangerous to society. These drugs were then placed into classes or schedules that categorize their particular dangers, from the most dangerous to the least. Listed below are the five drug schedules which categorize these dangerous drugs and their specific characteristics:

Schedule I

1. The drug has a high potential for abuse.
2. The drug has no currently accepted medical use in treatment in the United States.
3. There is a lack of safety for use of the drug or other substance under medical supervision.

Schedule II

1. The drug has a high potential for abuse.
2. The drug has a currently accepted medical use in treatment in the United States or a currently accepted medical use with severe restrictions.
3. Abuse of the drug may lead to severe psychological and physical dependence.

Schedule III

1. The drug has a potential for abuse less than the drugs contained in Schedules I and II.
2. The drug has a currently accepted medical use in treatment in the United States.
3. The drug may lead to moderate or low physical dependence or high psychological dependence.

Schedule IV

1. The drug has a low potential for abuse relative to the drugs found in Schedule II.
2. The drug has a currently accepted medical use for treatment in the United States.
3. The abuse of the drug may lead to limited physical dependence or psychological dependence relative to drugs found in Schedule III.

Schedule V

1. The drug has a low potential for abuse relative to drugs found in Schedule IV.
2. The drug has accepted medical use in treatment in the United States.
3. The abuse of the drug may lead to limited physical and psychological dependence relative to drugs in Schedule IV.

It would be too time consuming to attempt to describe all of the different drugs of abuse found on the street today. Some of these drugs are illegally manufactured by underground drug chemists, and some are made by legitimate pharmaceutical companies for specific types of medical treatment. Regardless of where the drugs come from, law enforcement officials over the years have observed the popularity of certain drugs over others. The following discussion will focus on primary drugs of abuse in today's society and what their different effects and characteristics are.

MARIJUANA

Chemical Name—*Cannabis sativa*
Classification—Schedule I, Mild Hallucinogen
Street Names—Pot, Reefer, Weed, Smoke, Grass, Bo

As indicated in Chapter 1, the use of marijuana throughout the world is certainly not a new phenomenon. Whether it is grown for recreational smoking or for its historic use as hemp to manufacture rope or clothing, this plant has made an absolute foothold in world history.

Marijuana is an attractive plant featuring broad-fingered leaves with sawtooth edges. The topside is a deep green, while the bottom is light green with a slight silver tint. The plant is one that seeds readily and flourishes in warm climates and, unless properly eradicated, it will continue to return year after year. In the height of the growing season, which is usually between August and mid-October, marijuana may grow up to six inches per day, reaching heights of twelve to sixteen feet.

Marijuana and its effects have been under study for quite some time, and there are always new findings about its effects on the body. According to Doctor Nicholas Pace, a founding director of the American Council on Marijuana and Other Psychoactive Drugs, over 420 different chemical properties have been identified in marijuana and it is likely that there could be many more. Doctor Pace further explains that many of the chemicals in marijuana are psychoactive and are considered to be extremely damaging to the so-called "fatty organs" of the body, such as the brain and the sex glands.

Some of these chemicals have been studied to one degree or another and some have not. One of the most active chemicals found in the plant is tetrahydrocannabinol, otherwise known as "THC." This is the chemical that, after reaching the brain, creates the euphoric or "high" effect sought by users. Proponents of legalizing marijuana claim that its use differs little from that of alcohol and should be legalized like alcohol. This comparison, however, is not really valid for a number of reasons.

A primary finding is that, for the most part, alcohol contains one chemical that, after ingested, is expelled from the body in about twelve hours. Marijuana, on the other hand, contains hundreds of chemicals, and the THC, which is only one of its chemical properties, seems to be attracted by these fatty tissues which may store it for up to three months. This, in turn, creates a severe cancer risk for the user (Fig. 1).

Although marijuana is classified as a mild hallucinogen, it seems to have a depressant-type effect on the central nervous system. The effects of the drug may cause drowsiness fatigue, and paranoia. Furthermore, it may create an intoxicating effect on the body, similar to that of alcohol, as users often complain of sleeplessness and a dry "cotton mouth" effect.

Where and how marijuana is grown will govern how potent its THC factor is. For example, a popular strain of domestically grown

Figure 1. Marijuana *(Cannabis sativa)* grows in abundance through the United States and can achieve heights of 12 to 16 feet. (Photo courtesy of the Oklahoma Bureau of Narcotics and Dangerous Drugs.)

marijuana labeled as "commercial marijuana" has an average THC content of 3 to 4 percent, while imported marijuana can be as high as 6 percent. A domestically grown strain of seedless marijuana known as "sinsemilla" originated several years ago in California. Although this particular type of marijuana is usually in demand on the street, it, for the most part, is not as common as commercial marijuana. It does, however, contain a high THC content that is reflected in its enormously high price tag. The care, attention, and climate of the growing marijuana plant will determine its degree of potency to one extent or another. This degree of potency will, in turn, dictate the street price of the manicured or finished product (see Chapter 11 on "Domestic Drug Sources").

Next, the street terms, prices, and common ways of packaging marijuana will be discussed. Consider first the weights and measurements commonly used in drug dealing:

General Measurements

1 Kilogram (kilo)—2.2 pounds
1 Pound—16 ounces
1 Ounce—28 grams

Prices for Domestic Grown Marijuana

1 Kilo – $1200 to $1800
1 Pound – $600 to $1200
1 Ounce – $75 to $120

Dated info see "High Times" for current prices

Prices of Imported Marijuana

1 Kilo – $1500 to $2000
1 Pound – $800 to $1400
1 Ounce – $85 to $130

Kilo and pound quantities of marijuana are usually packaged in plastic trash bags such as can be purchased at the supermarket.

Another form of packaging is the kilo "brick" (Fig. 2), which is simply a kilo of marijuana pressed into a rectangular brick by either using a home trash compactor or a homemade hydraulic press called a "bricker." These are then wrapped in colored or sometimes Mexican newspaper for transportation and distribution. In smuggling operations, the marijuana is usually delivered in "bales," which are usually about 100 pounds

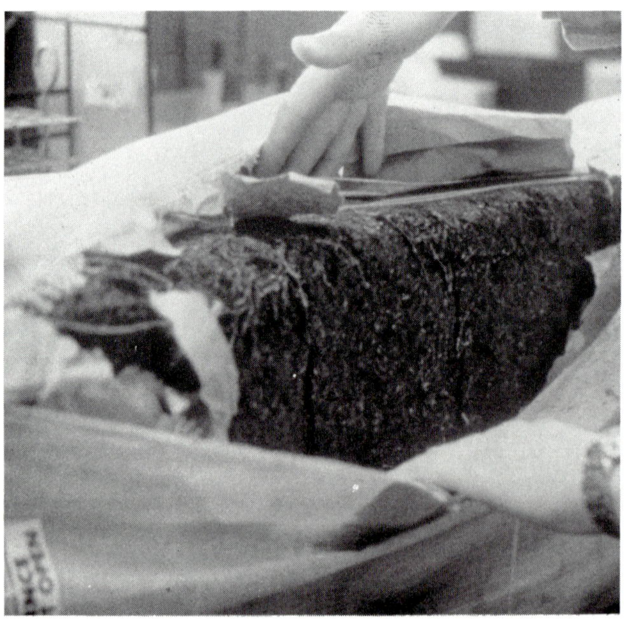

Figure 2. A 100-pound bail of marijuana seized in Tulsa, Oklahoma in 1985. Bails such as this are commonly found in smuggling operations. (Photo courtesy of the Oklahoma Bureau of Narcotics and Dangerous Drugs.)

each. As in the case of kilo bricks, this marijuana is usually tightly packed to take up less space in transportation. Obviously, the prices for imported marijuana are higher than that of domestically grown, with the exception of sinsemilla. The higher price accounts, of course, for a higher profit margin for the traffickers. The higher prices also provide dealers an ever-increasing incentive for continued involvement in the illegal drug trade.

Hashish
("Hash")

One substance produced from the marijuana plant, "hash," is made by extracting the potent resins from the plant. After the extraction process is completed, the finished product is a thick, chunky "block"-type substance in either a brown or a tan color. This contains a substantially higher THC content than even the best marijuana. Hash is usually smoked in a pipe or "bowl" and is extremely expensive when sold on the street. Small amounts (grams) of hash may sell for twenty to fifty dollars and are usually in high demand by users.

Other derivatives of the marijuana plant are hash oil and Thai sticks. All of these products are extremely potent but, for the most part, are less prevalent due to their high price tag and their difficulty to manufacture.

COCAINE

Chemical Name—Cocaine Hydrochloride
Classification—Schedule II, Stimulant
Street Names—Coke, Caine, Cola, Blow, Toot, Nose Candy, Girl, Flake

Cocaine is possibly the country's biggest drug of abuse in the 1980s. It is estimated that 22 million people have tried cocaine and that four million people are currently chronic or regular users of the substance.

Considered to be one of the most powerful stimulants known to man, its use during the last few years has claimed many victims, from comedian Richard Pryor's brush with death to the overdose death of comedian John Belushi in 1982, and the highly publicized cocaine trial of automaker John DeLorean in 1983.

In 1986, cocaine-related "sudden deaths" have claimed victims such as athletes Len Bias and Don Rogers in 1986.

The cocaine habit can cost the user an average of $100 dollars a day and may range up to $1,000–$3,000 per week for those who are addicted. Studies have indicated that the average age of a cocaine user has dropped in recent years from thirty-two to twenty-seven years old. This could be attributed to the fact that cocaine prices have fallen over the last few years and it is now more affordable to a broader market of users.

Users, for the most part, fall into the four following categories:

1. **Experimental.** Those who fall into this category do not use the drug consistently enough to become addicted but may easily fall into regular use due to peer pressure.
2. **Occasional.** This type of user maintains a consistency of cocaine use which falls short of chronic. Occasional use, however, may tend to build tolerance.
3. **Compulsive.** This user will not pass up a chance to take cocaine in any form and has established a heavy psychological dependence.
4. **Dependent.** The dependent user is addicted. This type of abuser has little control of his drug use and frequently finds himself in severe states of depression and financial hardship due to the excessive cost of his habit.

All of the above run some risk of the "sudden death" syndrome as experienced by Bias and Rogers, which makes cocaine an unpredictable and ever-threatening menace to all of its users. Other health risks associated with cocaine use are cerebral hemorrhage, cardiac arrest, and blood poisoning. This seems a high price to pay for a "high" that lasts only about twenty minutes (only about seven minutes when smoked or freebased).

When examining cocaine, let's first look at the plant itself, technically called erythroxylon coca. This is the plant that produces the alkaloids used in the synthesis of cocaine powder or hydrochloride. The coca plant is a bush-type plant which produces leaves as well as small red berries and a petite white-colored flower. The plant is finicky as to where it grows, requiring a proper combination of temperature, altitude, and humidity. While the climate in North America is not conducive to growing coca, the climate in the Andes of South America is most hospitable. Meeting the conditional growing requirements are countries such as Peru, Bolivia, and Columbia, just to name a few. More recently, South American countries farther south, such as Brazil, Chile, and Argentina, have been documented as harvesting large quantities of the coca plant.

The plant is harvested by local farm families that have produced coca leaves for generations. These families produce their crop on surprisingly small plots of land. The size of the land varies but averages around two-and-one-half acres per family. These coca farmers do not realize the enormous profits one might expect, but they do realize profits that almost triple what they would yield in growing a legitimate crop. The farmers are assisted by the entire family, from the oldest adult to the smallest child who help in gathering up the matured coca leaves. Many farmers have gained expertise in converting the leaf to the coca paste, known as "pasta" (see Chapter 4, "Profit Margin—The Allure of the Drug Business"). This pasta is ultimately converted to hydrochloride or powder form, which is then smuggled out of the growing countries for final processing into powder.

Cocaine, though originally classified as a narcotic, is now classified as a stimulant. It is considered extremely addictive and it reacts on the central nervous system. The drug is usually introduced into the bloodstream by one of the following methods:

1. Inhalation (sniffing)
2. Injection (booting)
3. Smoking (freebasing)

As pointed out earlier, the snorting of cocaine is the most common method of taking the drug. This is done by placing the cocaine in strips or lines on a flat surface such as a table. It is then snorted through a straw or a rolled up dollar bill and absorbed through the membranes in the nose and enters the bloodstream. The bloodstream then transports the substance directly to the brain, which produces an immediate reaction.

Once a user has acquired a tolerance for cocaine, he may then choose alternate ways of taking the drug. This could be achieved by either injecting it directly into the veins or by a more readily accepted method called "freebasing." This is done by mixing the cocaine with ether, kerosene, or one of many other substances and inhaling the smoke from the heated solution through a special pipe. Freebasing gives the user a much more intense feeling or "high" than sniffing but is considered by experts to be far more dangerous. The reason for this is that it requires much more cocaine to freebase than to snort and might "shock" the brain, causing instant death (Table 1). Since smoking cocaine requires more product, it also takes much more money to afford it, sometimes two to three times as much money.

Table 1

Cocaine Related Deaths in the United States (1981-1984)

1981:	334
1982:	239
1983:	349
1984:	617

Source: 1984 Narcotics Intelligence Estimate. National Narcotics Intelligence Consumers Committee.

These are the typical "street" prices of cocaine in various quantities:

1 Kilo—approximately $40,000 to $50,000
1 Pound—approximately $22,000 to $26,000
1 Ounce—approximately $1800 to $2200
1 Gram—approximately $100 to $150
1/4 Gram—approximately $35

The prices of retail cocaine may vary across the country for a number of reasons. Some of these reasons are outlined below:

1. Where it is purchased affects the price. Buying cocaine in the United States is much more expensive than purchasing it in South America. For example, a kilo of cocaine in Colombia could be as cheap as $5,000. Even the purchasing of cocaine in a coastal city such as Houston or Miami could be cheaper than an inland city like Kansas City, depending on the business relationships of the traffickers.
2. How many times the substance has been "cut" (i.e., its purity) has a direct relationship to its price. This is difficult to determine, however, because most cocaine dealers claim that their product is of high quality. According to the National Institute on Drug Abuse, the cocaine that ends up in the hands of the consumer ranges widely from 12 percent to 75 percent pure.
3. Its lack of availability in a particular area might cause dealers to charge a higher price for a drug than when it is more readily available.

Cocaine in kilos or ounce quantities is usually packaged in clear plastic bags to enable prospective buyers to inspect the contents. A gram or a quarter gram (also called a "quarter paper") may be packaged in either clear plastic packets, aluminum foil packets, or a specially folded piece of paper called a "bindle."

Bindles are the most popular form of packaging cocaine in smaller quantities (usually one gram). These are small, white paper packets specially folded to safeguard against the spillage of any of the powder.

Crack

A freebase form of cocaine which has become popular because of its high potency and relatively "low" price is referred to on the street as "crack." This is a small, tan, rock-looking substance (Fig. 37). Crack may sell for $10–$50 on the street and is affordable to users who do not have a lot of money to spend, such as adolescents and even children. This intense form of cocaine is now commonly found on the streets of most major cities in the United States and in particular in the inner cities.

Figure 3. "Crack" is a new non-volatile form of freebase cocaine which sells for $10 to $50 per vile on the street. (Photo courtesy of the Dallas, Texas Police Department.)

According to a June 16, 1986, *Newsweek* article on crack and crime, the smoking of crack creates such intense ups and downs for the user that its use may result in a powerful chemical dependency within two weeks.

Due to the increase of crack use in the larger cities, "crack houses" have become popular with users and have posed many problems for law enforcement officers. The crack house is a house, apartment or private club where a user can both purchase the drug and use it on the premises. In some instances, the buyer only can purchase the drug but is denied entry and is not allowed to see faces of dealers. Many of these "crack houses" are fortified with steel doors and door jams, as well as bars on the windows to defeat entry by police or rip-off artists.

The real danger of "crack" is that many potential "crack" users are "experimental" or "occasional" cocaine users rather than chronic users. Since the users have not yet built up a tolerance for cocaine as many freebasers have, the chance of overdose or even death is extremely high.

For the most part, cocaine is a very expensive drug whose popularity has dramatically increased in recent years. For a long time cocaine was considered to be affordable by only the rich, but now due to its new street form "crack," society sees its use at almost every social and economic level. "Crack" is made from cocaine in a number of different ways, but one common method is to mix a quantity of cocaine with an equal quantity of baking soda or ammonia. Next, the mixture is dissolved in water (cocaine is water-soluble). The solution is then poured into a container and then goes through an alternating process of heating and cooling until a gummy substance begins to form. This substance is then poured through a filter, which in many cases is a paper towel or silk scarf, and the residue collects on the filter. This residue is "crack," and it is then scraped off the filter and allowed to dry before it is chopped up and placed in small designer bottles for distribution.

This has become a drug of choice for those who like to freebase cocaine. Because the process does not include the use of volatile chemicals such as ether, it virtually eliminates the dangers of fire and explosion encountered in traditional freebasing. It is estimated, however, that the potency of "crack" averages from 70 to 90 percent pure, which adds to its degree of danger.

METHAMPHETAMINE/AMPHETAMINE

Classification—Schedule II, Stimulant
Street Terms—Crank, Crystal, Speed, Blue Rock Crystal

Along with the popularity of cocaine are stimulants known as methamphetamine or amphetamine. Even though these drugs are gaining popularity, they still do not have the wide-spread appeal of cocaine. The differences between methamphetamine and amphetamine are so subtle that they can be differentiated from one another primarily by chemical analysis. Both drugs are white or off-white colored powders and their effects are very similar to one another.

Although a large percentage of these drugs are legally manufactured, much amphetamine and methamphetamine is made in clandestine laboratories by chemists or "cooks" who have acquired expertise in chemistry. Outlaw motorcycle gangs play a significant role in the manufacturing of methamphetamine and amphetamine in the United States and Canada, and it is estimated that these groups control up to 40 percent of the nation's supply of the drug.

These drugs may be snorted like cocaine, but more commonly methamphetamine, also known as "crank," is considered "shooting dope" and is injected by its users. The term "speed freak" is commonly associated with those who are chronic users of methamphetamine and amphetamine; they are frequently thin and frail with open sores, as well as runny eyes and nose cavities.

The price of methamphetamine powder is approaching that of cocaine but is still substantially less. A gram may cost the user anywhere from $75 to $100 while an ounce will cost from $1,400 to $2,000 each (see Chapter 11, "Domestic Drug Sources").

LSD

Chemical Name—Lysergic Acid Diethylamide
Classification—Schedule I, Hallucinogen
Street Names—Acid, Microdot, Blotter acid, Window pane, LSD-25

The experimental use of LSD in the late 1950s has evolved into a continuing health threat in the 1980s. With abuse trends that fluctuate every few years from virtual unpopularity to one of the most sought-after street drugs, LSD continually seems to captivate drug users throughout the country despite its historically bad publicity.

All forms of LSD are illegal throughout the country, and most criminal penalties are severe. The drug is illegally manufactured in clandestine laboratories and appears to take many different forms when sold on the street. This is because, when synthesized, it is a clear liquid resembling water and can be placed on anything such as tablets or paper or even in drinks.

Most commonly, LSD comes in a tablet form called microdot acid. These tablets are so tiny that they might easily fit under a fingernail and are subsequently easy to conceal by dealers.

When sold on the street, these tablets or "hits" usually sell for four or five dollars each and are commonly nicknamed "orange barrels," "purple haze," and other "candy" sounding names.

"Blotter acid" is a popular form of LSD which also sells for about five dollars each. This is a number of small cartoon characters printed on a piece of paper to which LSD has been added. The characters of the cartoon vary from time to time, but have included pictures of Mickey Mouse, Snoopy, and Goofy. These pictures are either licked or eaten by consumers.

HEROIN

Chemical Name—Diacetylmorphine
Classification—Schedule I, Narcotic/Opiate
Street Names—Heroin, Smack, Junk, Horse, Boy, "H", China White, Mexican Brown

As observed in the drug legacy chapter, opiates and their derivatives have been a thorn in the side of mankind since early recorded history. Its use prevails in the 1980s in large proportions, predominantly in the inner-city areas of larger metropolitan cities. Considered for the most part to be a drug of the poor and oppressed, society has seen many examples of heroin use by celebrities, athletes, and the socially affluent.

Approximately 70 percent of the heroin that comes into the United States is white in color and is exported from Asia. The remaining 30 percent is light brown and is brought in from Mexico.

Heroin is a chemical derivative of the poppy plant known as *Papaver somniferum,* which, like the coca plant, does not grow successfully in the United States. It does, however, grow in abundance throughout Mexico and parts of Asia. This small flowered plant has been the cause of untold misery, disease, and death throughout the world and has even caused nations to go to war with each other (Table 2). The plant itself produces a bulb which, when harvested, secretes a black tar-like substance that is raw opium. It is this raw opium that is used to process refined heroin.

Table 2

Heroin-Morphine Related Deaths in the United States (1981-1984)

1981:	930
1982:	991
1983:	800
1984:	1,046

Source: 1984 Narcotics Intelligence Estimate. National Narcotics Intelligence Consumers Committee.

Even though opium itself can be smoked, heroin is still a more popular form that many opiate abusers prefer. Being an opiate, heroin is an extremely addictive drug, both psychologically and physically. It does, however, provide the user with a much sought-after "high" which has been compared to that of a roller-coaster ride.

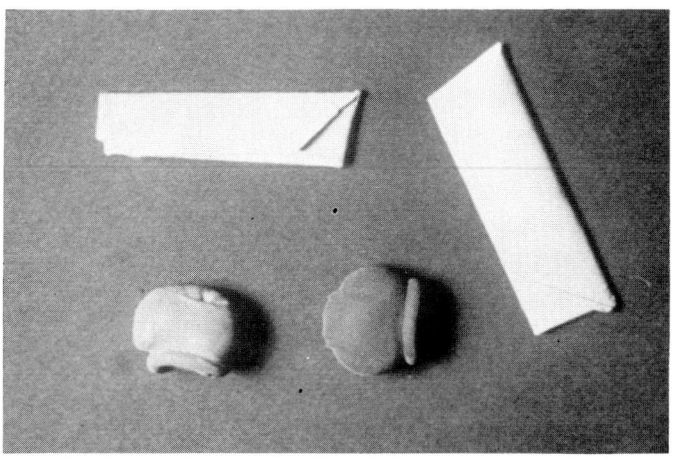

Figure 4. Paper "bindles" commonly used to transport gram quantities of cocaine and other powders, and balloons used to transport heroin. (Photo courtesy of the Oklahoma Bureau of Narcotics and Dangerous Drugs Control.)

There are several primary reasons why such widespread abuse of heroin exists over other types of drugs. These are listed as follows:

1. It is usually cheaper than other types of powdered drugs, e.g., cocaine, amphetamine.

2. It is plentiful in the areas where the abuse is greatest, such as ghettos and economically depressed areas.
3. Because of its addictive properties, users might become addicted with chronic use, and dealers may attempt to "hook" potential users by initially offering them freebies.
4. The peer-pressure factor in economically depressed areas is every bit as strong as in other areas of society and is a significant contributing factor in heroin abuse.

The heroin trade is an extremely lucrative one involving many different countries (see Chapter 3, "Foreign Drug Sources"). Those countries responsible for manufacturing heroin (and cocaine for that matter) recognize their problem but blame the United States for providing a market for the drug in the first place. The United States has had, and still has, the dubious distinction of being the world's largest consumer of drugs, both legal and illegal (Table 3).

Table 3

Heroin Consumption in the United States, 1981-1984 (Metric Tons)

1981:	3.85
1982:	5.47
1983:	6.04
1984:	5.97

Source: 1984 Narcotics Intelligence Estimate. National Narcotics Intelligence Consumers Committee.

PCP

Chemical Name—Phencyclidine
Classification—Schedule I, Hallucinogen
Street Names— Water, Wack, Angel Dust, Shirms, Shirm Sticks, Super Cools, Jet Fuel

PCP is a hallucinogen which is synthetically manufactured. Although once used as an animal tranquilizer, the drug is primarily seen nowadays as a recreational drug illegally produced on the street. Available in various forms such as powder, liquid, and occasionally tablets,

PCP is manufactured entirely in clandestine laboratories and is still seeing a significant user market on the street.

Because of a bad overall reputation on the street, PCP is often sold as other drugs such as cannabinol, LSD, or THC.

Even though the drug acts as a tranquilizer on animals, it has a devastating hallucinogenic and unpredictable effect on its human victims. Lured to the drug by claims of euphoria, its users are usually stricken with severe, intense, and sometimes violent hallucinations. Oddly enough, the drug seems to endure periods of abstinence by its users due to general public awareness of its dangers, but periods of newfound popularity among users seem to come again.

Severe psychosis has been associated with the use of PCP, even to the point where permanent brain damage is likely for chronic users. Another inherent danger associated with the drug is a potential for violent behavior by its users. Often, when police officers attempt to arrest individuals under the influence of PCP, they discover that the arrestee exhibits extreme strength and agility, as well as a propensity to resist arrest.

The drug does, in fact, produce an absolute effect of strength in its users and tends to minimize pain to the extent that the user may not initially feel pain associated with gunshot wounds or broken bones.

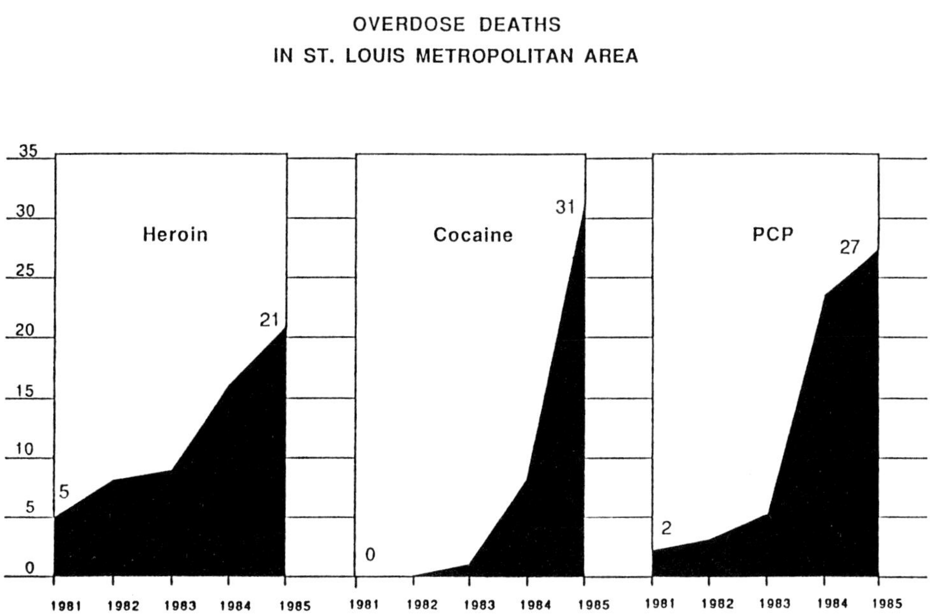

Figure 5. This chart shows the dramatic increase in drug overdose deaths in St. Louis, Missouri between 1981 and 1985. (Chart courtesy of the State of Missouri Bureau of Narcotics and Dangerous Drugs.)

PHARMACEUTICAL DRUGS

Pharmaceutical drugs are those that are legally manufactured for legitimate medical use in treatment. Many pharmaceutical firms throughout the world manufacture almost any type of drug imaginable. These drugs usually fall into two general categories: those that are sold over the counter and those that are controlled. Over-the-counter drugs are those which may be purchased without a prescription, such as aspirin, decongestants, and caffeine diet pills, while controlled drugs cannot be dispensed without a doctor's prescription and are otherwise illegal to possess.

For the purposes of this chapter, we will concern ourselves with those drugs which are controlled. Some of these drugs such as tranquilizers are relatively mild, while others such as Demerol and Dilaudid, cause a more intense and potentially dangerous reaction to the body.

Often, the risk of overdose or death is compounded when some drugs, particularly barbiturates, are mixed with alcohol or other drugs creating a synergistic effect on the body.

It is difficult to list all of the various pharmaceuticals that are abused on the street, because the availability of this type of drug largely depends on its particular source of diversion. This is to say that there may not be an abundance of diazepam (Valium) available unless there is an individual on the street actively involved in either drugstore burglaries, "script walking," or another scheme to obtain drugs by fraud or deceit. Although many pharmaceutical drugs are also manufactured in clandestine laboratories, much of their availability is attributed to acts of criminal diversion.

Typically, however, some of the more sought-after pharmaceutical drugs on the street are:

Stimulants – Ritalin
Dexedrine
Preludin

Depressants – Valium (Diazepam)
Tuinal
Phenobarbital

Narcotics – Percodan
Dilaudid
Talwin

The drugs listed above are only a few of the more popularly abused pharmaceutical drugs. As a rule of thumb, however, it would be safe to say that most any pharmaceutical drugs would be easily sold on the street if offered to potential buyers.

One of the biggest problems associated with the abuse of pharmaceutical drugs is that a significant percentage of abuse is done by those who have legitimately acquired the drugs through prescriptions. Some of this abuse is intentional, and some of it is inadvertent or accidental, but still accounts for hundreds of drug-related deaths every year.

Abusers of the depressant category (especially barbiturates) often find themselves addicted in relatively little time. Another problem associated with the taking of these drugs is that tolerance frequently occurs. This means that it becomes necessary to increase the dosage of the drug to still obtain the desired effects. This occurrence is true for a number of different drugs of abuse. Those who desire to take stimulant pharmaceuticals also frequently experience a period of great depression, called "crashing."

About 88 percent of all pharmaceutical amphetamines are prescribed for weight control, while other conditions treated by amphetamines are narcolepsy and hyperkinetic behavioral disorders in children.

To positively identify a capsule or table believed to be a pharmaceutical, check a *Physicians' Desk Reference* (PDR), which is published once a year. This text offers descriptions and photographs of commonly prescribed and dangerous drugs that are legally manufactured.

DESIGNER DRUGS

The term and general concept of designer drugs is a relatively new one in the 1980s. It is a term which describes clandestinely manufactured chemicals which, when sold on the street, supposedly provide the user with the desirable effects of controlled drugs without any of the negative effects. Furthermore, these chemicals are touted as being perfectly legal, and in many cases they are.

Most state and federal laws specifically describe the various controlled substances in detail. Laws not only set forth the schedule and different penalties associated with the drug but identify the exact chemical name for the substance.

What these drug manufacturers have done is altered some of the chemical components of certain controlled drugs, actually changing the specific chemical name, making it a substance that is not listed in criminal law. In essence, this makes the "new drug" legal. Federal law has attempted to schedule some of these substances, but as soon as laws are passed, the chemists change the composition of the drug to make it "legal" again.

Some states such as Oklahoma have addressed the problem with state legislation called "designer drug laws." Oklahoma's law, for the most part, does not name specific drugs but makes distribution of a substance illegal if it meets certain criterion. Oklahoma's law is briefly described here.

A drug is illegal to possess or distribute if it:

1. Has like or similar physiological or psychological qualities of an already existing controlled substance.
2. Has no accepted medical use in treatment in the United States.
3. Has a potential for abuse.

"Ecstasy" is a designer drug that has seen considerable use since 1985 and, before it was outlawed, was even given away as a door prize at certain nightclubs in Dallas, Texas. Assuming other names such as "Eve," "XTC," and "Turbo," it is alleged to be a "party drug" which releases inhibitions and makes a person more open and sociable. Its effects are reportedly similar to those of LSD but without the negative side effects such as "flashbacks" and "bad trips."

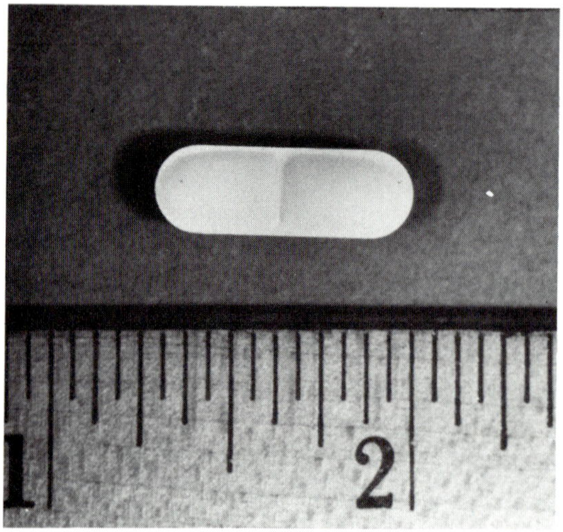

Figure 6. Ecstasy, also called XTC or Turbo, is a designer drug with many of the same dangers of LSD. (Photo courtesy of the Dallas, Texas Police Department.)

The drug was originally shaped like an over-the-counter caplet that is white in color, but it has also been distributed in a round tablet form. It usually sells for around twenty dollars each and is frequently broken in half and shared between two users. The technical name for this drug is methylenedioxymethamphetamine, or simply, "MDMA," sharing many of the same chemical components as its 1960s predecessor, MDA (a close cousin to LSD). The difference in the two is that a "methel" chemical component was added to the original MDA formula to change the name of the substance.

"China White" heroin is an old label for a new designer drug that is not actually heroin at all. The new China White seems to have originated in California and has claimed many deaths and overdoses, in the Orange County area in particular. The most frightening aspect of the drug is that it causes tragic "Hodgkin's disease" type symptoms, ranging from partial paralysis to death. The primary component in this designer drug is a compound called 3-methyl-fentanyl or alpha fentanyl, a white powder with a potency of 1,000 times that of morphine (or higher). All a chemist has to do is manufacture just "one" batch of this chemical and, because of its potency, he will have enough chemical product to sell for the rest of his drug-dealing career.

INHALANTS

Inhalants are a group of diverse volatile substances that people do not normally think of as drugs. Most of these substances are basically household articles that possess dangerous and mind-altering properties.

As the name implies, abusers inhale the fumes from the articles and achieve a high similar to that of alcohol or sedatives, although the results can be much more rapidly obtained.

The most likely item of abuse is anything found in a spray can such as paint, hair spray, and gasoline. The lead component in these substances is considered to be the most toxic element associated with the sniffing of inhalants. The abuse of this type of drug may cause instant death or other health risks such as vomiting, nausea, or even liver and kidney damage.

CHAPTER 3

FOREIGN DRUG SOURCES

THE ESCALATION of illicit drug manufacturing and production activities within the United States is an ever-increasing problem to law enforcement agencies. As difficult as it is to police these domestic criminal activities, it is nearly impossible to control the even greater production of drugs in foreign countries. This chapter discusses why foreign drug traffic seems to be on the rise.

Most illicit drugs consumed in the United States are cultivated or manufactured outside the country. The "Golden Crescent," for instance, is comprised of three Southwest Asian countries: Iran, Pakistan, and Afghanistan. These countries are poppy- and cannabis-producing countries responsible for the production of most of the world's heroin and a significant percentage of the world's hashish.

Southwest Asian heroin is produced in clandestine laboratories primarily in western Iran and eastern Turkey. It is then smuggled by Turkish nationals to established markets throughout Europe and the Netherlands.

Up until the late 1970s, a group of opium-producing countries called the "Golden Triangle" produced the majority of the world's heroin (Fig. 7). These countries are Laos, Burma, and Thailand and, although second in world heroin production, together produced an estimated 600 tons of opium in 1986. Traffickers, also using the Netherlands as a main distribution area, acquire processed heroin from conversion laboratories in Bangkok and Hong Kong.

Cocaine seems to come primarily from South America, where the use and cultivation of coca has been accepted for generations. Countries such as Colombia, Peru, and Bolivia have been producing coca and cocaine for so long that it is likely the national economy of each country is strongly enhanced by drug revenues.

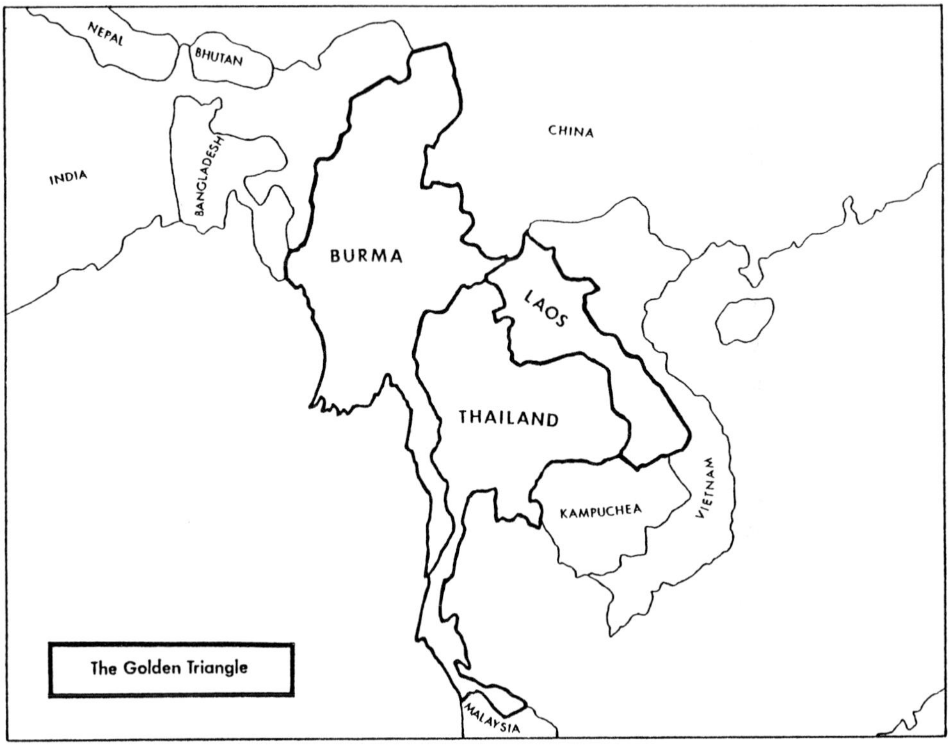

Figure 7. Map of Golden Triangle.

In 1986, however, pursuant to a request from the Bolivian government, the United States sent troops to Bolivia to assist in a series of raids aimed at clandestine cocaine laboratories and coca plantations. One indication of the success of these raids is the recent discovery of cocaine-processing laboratories in Costa Rica, Panama, and other areas of Central America. These labs could indicate a displacement of cocaine production activities to new areas where law enforcement is considered lacking and where immigration policies are liberal. It is hoped that cooperative international policing such as this will become commonplace in future global drug-suppression efforts and will continue to displace and deter future drug production and smuggling activity.

Marijuana, although cultivated worldwide, is one of Mexico's chief illegally produced substances, along with brown heroin. Many countries that are not considered major drug producers like Mexico still assist in the smuggling of illegal drugs. These countries are termed "transshipment countries" and are frequently used as stop-off points for already produced drugs or drugs that require final processing. For example, heroin produced in Mexico commonly transits the Yucatan or Belize before entering the United States. Cocaine, produced in Colombia, may frequently pass through Mexico en route to the United States. Traffickers realize that U.S. authorities suspect packages entering the United States from known source countries, due to their international drug reputation. So, by transporting the package through other countries, theoretically, detection may be avoided.

Countries in the "Golden Crescent" often use transshipment countries such as France, Spain, Germany, and England to expedite their exportation operations. Even though this is a fairly innovative way to smuggle drugs, authorities are now becoming increasingly aware of these techniques in their detection processes.

Let's now take a closer look at a few of the primary source countries throughout the world.

MEXICO

Mexico continues to be one of the world's most formidable and consistent suppliers of illicit substances to the United States. With traditional and escalating involvement in heroin and marijuana production, Mexico remains one of the key drug source countries in the world. Confirming this hypothesis was a 1984 raid of a Chihuahua marijuana operation that netted over 10,000 tons of illegal weed destined for the United States. This raid has since raised further questions regarding the extent of Mexico's political and governmental involvement in this illegal business.

The drug traffic along the 2,000-mile Mexican border is believed to account for one-third of the marijuana and heroin entering the United States. These overall statistics rank mexico as the second largest producer of marijuana in the world (next to Colombia). Furthermore, according to U.S. Customs authorities, the amount of cocaine seized at the Mexican border increased 81 percent from 1983 to 1984. As previously discussed, it is believed that the majority of the seized cocaine, however, is not being manufactured in Mexico but merely transits through the country from South America. The amount of heroin seized at the border during this same period, however, remained virtually consistent with previous years.

Other drug-related problems in Mexico as mentioned are increasing indications of internal governmental corruption in the illicit drug trade.

With the murders of U.S. Drug Enforcement agent Enrique Camarena Salazar and his colleague, Mexican pilot Alfredo Zavala Avelar, in February 1985, evidence of political and governmental criminal involvement has become increasingly evident and poses new dangers to those who choose to combat drug trafficking in Mexico.

COLOMBIA

Colombia has the dubious distinction of being the world's largest drug producer and supplier. This fact could be attributed to its strategic geographical location on the South American continent as well as its vast experience in the traditional cultivation and production of cocaine and marijuana. These two drugs have an estimated value to the Colombian economy of about $1.5 billion annually.

Colombia itself is a major transshipment center for coca leaves and coca pasta produced in Peru and Bolivia. The traffickers, over the years, have acquired keen cultivation, chemical synthesis, and smuggling techniques that are put to the test every year. According to *The Encyclopedia of Drug Abuse* by O'Brien and Cohen, Colombia is probably responsible for 70 percent of the cocaine entering the United States and over 50 percent of the entire world's supply. Furthermore, it is estimated by U.S. authorities that the cocaine produced in Colombia and smuggled into the United States has a street value of $29 billion yearly.

Colombia's marijuana-producing enterprises also furnish about 70 percent of the U.S. user market. The degree of drug dealing in Colombia is such big business that money to purchase drugs is often packaged in bundles of one hundred dollar bills, which are weighed by the dealers rather than counted.

Historically, most of the drugs produced in Colombia pass through the East Coast port areas, south Florida, and the Gulf of Mexico, but due to recent drug task force concentration in these areas, smugglers are seeking new, more inland ports of entry for their products.

While cocaine is such big business in Colombia, it is interesting to note that the country has outlawed three of the primary chemical precursors considered essential for processing coca into cocaine. Production of these chemicals, ether, hydrochloric acid, and acetone, was made illegal on January 4, 1983, by the Colombian Minister of Economic Development in an effort to curb production of cocaine. The traffickers, however, are usually successful in smuggling these chemicals from the United States and other countries.

Recently, there have been documented reports of terrorist guerrilla groups aiding traffickers by providing a network of guards for cocaine-processing facilities. These terrorists work for the traffickers as a source of income to pay for illegal arms shipments.

PERU

For more than two thousand years Peruvians have been growing and chewing coca for medicinal and recreational uses. Today, the Peruvian government licenses and permits substantial cultivation of coca for traditional domestic use as well as pharmaceutical purposes. Despite governmental controls, yearly coca production has expanded to an estimated 50,000 metric tons which drastically exceed the legally allotted 14,000 tons.

The growing of coca greatly enhances the already weak Peruvian economy. Even though the farmers work on lots averaging only 2.5 acres each, the coca plant is often their principle and only income for thousands of farmers who earn up to three times more income growing coca than legitimate crops. Coca is an attractive plant to farm because of the following three factors:

1. It is a deep-rooted plant with a life span of about thirty years.
2. It can be harvested about three to six times a year.
3. It can flourish in poor-quality soil that may be unsuitable for other crops.

Although farming coca to sell to cocaine producers might be attractive to farmers, it presents a major problem for others. The freebasing of cocaine in the 1980s is a growing problem in Peru as in the United States. Peruvian drug users freebase coca paste, which presents numerous health risks due to impurities such as cement, kerosene, and large amounts of cocaine alkaloids.

The drug abuse problem became so severe that in 1981 a five-year coca eradication and enforcement plan was implemented by the Bureau of International Narcotics Matters (INM) to diversify agricultural development. It was reported that by 1982 about 5 percent of coca cultivation had been abandoned and certain other ongoing cultivations were not being completed.

BOLIVIA

The cultivation and consumption of coca has been traditional for centuries in Bolivia, and, along with Colombia, Bolivia is responsible for most of the world's supply of cocaine. An estimated 23,000 farm families grow coca in Bolivia on small acreages of land that, as in Peru, are usually about 2.5 acres.

Coca leaf and cocaine production in Bolivia is worth some $600 million, totaling more than all legitimate exports in the country. Furthermore, approximately 650 million people profit from the illegal cocaine trade, averaging $3,200 per year. This is considered a small fortune in a poverty-stricken country such as Bolivia.

Like Peru's coca production, much of the raw coca base and coca leaves produced in Bolivia is processed in neighboring Colombia. The expertise necessary to refine the coca pasta into cocaine powder or hydrochloride, however, is now much more prevalent in Bolivia than ever before due to recent drug crackdowns in Colombia.

Drug eradication and enforcement efforts traditionally flounder in source countries such as Bolivia because of the country's weak political and governmental structure. Bolivia, for instance, has averaged one government per year since the republic was founded in 1825. Each time the United States begins to gain ground in joint drug-suppression efforts with Bolivia, a political change takes place and efforts to resume coca leaf control must begin all over again (Table 4).

Table 4

Estimated Cocaine Production

	Peru	**Bolivia**	**Colombia**	**Ecuador**	**Brazil**
1983 Estimated Coca Leaf Yield (Metric Tons)	30,000-60,000	25,000-40,000	12,000-14,000	--	--
Maximum Cocaine (HCL) Capacity (Metric Tons)	60-120	50-80	25-27	--	--
Total Cocaine (HCL) Production: 135-227 Metric Tons					
1984 Estimated Coca Leaf Yield (Metric Tons)	50,000-70,000	42,000-63,000	12,000-14,000	1,000	?
Maximum Cocaine (HCL) Capacity (Metric Tons)	100-140	84-126	24-28	2	?
Total Cocaine (HCL) Production: 210-296 Metric Tons					

Source: President's Commission on Organized Crime, *America's Drug Habit,* Report to the President and the Attorney General, March 1986.

IRAN

Opium use has been a widespread problem in Iran for generations. It is eaten or smoked and is usually used in conjunction with hashish and marijuana, which are also produced within the country.

It is estimated that there are 350,000 to 500,000 heroin addicts in Iran, which has a population of 40 million. Compare this addiction ratio to that of the United States, which has an addict population of approximately 500,000 out of a total population of 200 million.

Before the revolution, Iran responded favorably to requests by other countries to cut back on opium production for exportation. Other constructive steps had been taken by the Iranian government, such as:

1. In 1955, a ban on opium production was imposed.
2. In 1969, the cultivation of the opium poppy plant was made a governmental monopoly under very strict laws that imposed harsh fines for possession, trafficking, exporting and importing of opium or hashish.

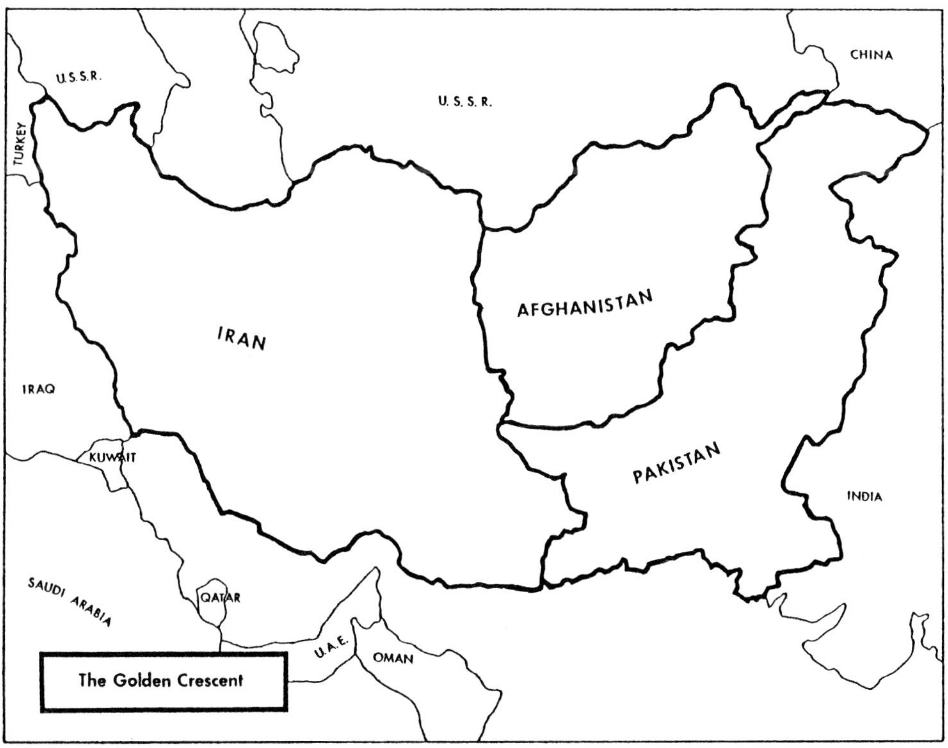

Figure 8. Map of Golden Crescent.

As the Shah's hold on Iran began to weaken, law and order became less prevalent and the ban on illicit opium production began to be ignored. Consequently, exportation of the drug began to increase. In 1979, the Shah, whose government worked so hard in drug suppression, was overthrown by the Ayatollah Khomeini regime. The police and military forces who previously enforced the drug laws were reassigned to other duties such as internal security. Furthermore, many of those who had staffed law enforcement units became outcasts and were considered enemies of the people.

Iran is now aligned with Pakistan and Afghanistan in the "Golden Crescent" (Fig. 8) and is a major producer of heroin, hashish, and morphine base for their many clandestine laboratories.

TURKEY

The use of opium, hashish, and marijuana have long been a tradition in Turkey. Actually, the customary use of drugs is so far embedded in Turkish society that there is no longer a negative social stigma attached to it. Heroin use is rare in Turkey, even though the customary use of opium flourishes. Opium is usually smoked, eaten, or chewed in a gum which is a raw opium product.

Back in the 1920s the New Republic sought to revamp the nation's laws and practices, and programs were established to end many of the old customs such as the use of hash and opium. This proved to be an effort in futility as the use of opium continued to increase, as did opium smuggling practices.

In 1971, national legislation was passed to ban the production of opium despite attempts for its appeal. This law is still in effect and has caused some economic hardships that have led to farming compensation programs in the country. These programs are not easy successes, because most of the poppy farms must be rehabilitated and the social and economic structure of whole provinces must be reorganized.

The laws governing sale, possession, and trafficking of drugs in Turkey are extremely harsh. In the case of cocaine, morphine, hash, or heroin, the penalty can be life in prison, and Turkish jails have a reputation for extremely uncomfortable conditions.

Despite past bans on the cultivation of the opium poppy, many Turks are still actively involved in the illicit drug market. Turkey has become a major transshipment country for heroin produced in Pakistan and Iran (the Golden Crescent). Turkish nationals also play a significant role in the refining and trafficking of imported opiates through other transshipment countries such as Spain and the Federal Republic of Germany.

JAMAICA

Jamaica, like so many other countries throughout the world, has seen drug and alcohol use for many years. The use of marijuana, or as Jamaican's call it, "ganja," has been going on for over one hundred years and is thought to have been introduced by laborers from India (Table 5).

Table 5

Marijuana Importation

Colombia	75%
Jamaica	10%
Mexico	8%
Domestic	7%

Source: Drug Enforcement Administration, Drug Enforcement, Summer 1982 (Washington D.C.: Dept. of Justice).

Historically, ganja was only used by certain small groups of people, but now its use has spread to all segments of society. The use of ganja is so widespread that it has been suggested that it is the basis for the Jamaican economy. Ganja, in fact, has been against the law in Jamaica since 1913, but its use is so widespread that many law enforcement officers turn their backs on the problem, permitting cultivation, distribution and possession. Authorities estimate that up to 60 percent of the island's total population use ganja on a regular basis. Its use plays a particular role in the lives of the Rastafarians. Reggae music, made popular by this group, depicts drug use as normal and encourages the use of ganja in the musical lyrics. The women and children of Jamaica have been known to consume ganja in a beverage called green tea. To many people, this is a more social form of ingestion than smoking the drug.

Jamaican gangs have posed a new law enforcement problem in many major American cities such as Boston, New York, Washington, Baltimore,

Philadelphia, Atlanta, Kansas City, Dallas, and Houston. These gangs are linked by law enforcement authorities to drug trafficking and gun running and are believed to be responsible for hundreds of murders.

With possible mafia affiliations, these gangs are considered even more dangerous than the Colombian "cocaine cowboys" of the early 1980s, who gained notoriety for public machine gun slayings in Miami.

INDIA

India is rapidly emerging as a major source country for heroin production. Already, India is the world's largest producer of raw gum opium which is "legally" used to manufacture drugs such as morphine and other addictive drugs.

The national government, which regulates the opium poppy industry, pays farmers up to $25 a kilogram (2.2 lbs.) but is reducing its production goals because of a decline in exports. As well as major drug manufacturing within the country, India is also emerging as a major transshipment country for illicit drugs produced in Burma and Pakistan.

A U.S. State Department report estimated that India legally exported 700 metric tons of opium in 1986, much of which went to the United States (Table 6). The U.S. Drug Enforcement Administration estimates that 51 percent of the heroin consumed in the United States comes from Southwest Asia. Other sources estimate that as much as half of the heroin in the United States is brought in from India alone, yet opium production is being spurred by local consumption levels rather than increased demand here in the United States. The United States Drug Enforcement Administration has recently considered dispatching additional drug agents to India to assist the Indian government in drug enforcement efforts.

Table 6

Heroin Importation

Burma, Laos, Thailand	15%
Iran, Pakistan, Afganistan	60%
Mexico	25%

CHAPTER 4

PROFIT MARGIN—THE ALLURE OF THE DRUG BUSINESS

THE OBVIOUS and single most powerful motive for drug trafficking activity is the making of money . . . easy money. Revenues generated from drug trafficking might seem to be easily earned, but many people fail to realize the many personal concerns and business-related problems that accompany drug trafficking activities. The following is a checklist of considerations concerning drug traffickers in their chosen occupation:

1. The possibility of a police informer knowing of the operation.
2. The possibility of other drug dealers stealing their supply ("stash") of drugs.
3. The possibility of being murdered during a drug transaction for drugs or money.
4. The possibility that drugs purchased might be nothing more than storebought baking soda or an equivalent that merely resembles the actual drugs.
5. The possibility of being caught and sent to the penitentiary.
6. The probability of dealing with people who are virtual strangers.
7. The probability of associating on a regular basis with people who carry weapons and who have committed violent crimes.

This chapter is concerned with the allure of profit in the illegal drug trade and will attempt to explain why there is such a significant profit margin in drug-trafficking activities. Many factors contribute to the degree of profit margin in each drug transaction.

The following four considerations should help illustrate the different variables involved:

1. *The Drug's Place of Origin.* This plays a significant role in the overall profit scheme, because so many middlemen are required to not only manufacture the drug but to transport (smuggle) it to the United States. The premise is simple: the more people involved, the more people need to get paid.

2. *The Type of Drug.* This factor could very well have a direct bearing on the degree of profit in a drug transaction, because some drugs can be adulterated (cut) more easily than others. It can be assumed that most powders have experienced a "cutting" process with each dealer who comes into contact with the drug.

3. *A Close Buyer-Seller Relationship.* A drug dealer who has dealt closely with a buyer for a considerable length of time is much more likely to give that person a lower price on a drug than someone who is yet untested. Suspicion clouds every drug transaction and drug operation to the extent that dealers will usually sacrifice a percentage of their projected profits in return for the peace of mind in dealing with a "friend."

4. *Individual Dealing Practices.* The individual dealing practices of the buyer (and the seller) also play a large role in drug profits. For some dealers, a reputation for good quality dope is the most important consideration in business. This individual usually deals with established buyers who are familiar to the dealer and whose return business he wishes to keep. Other dealers might "play the numbers" and sell indiscriminantly to many buyers with whom they are not familiar and may never see again. This type will most likely sell a drug whose quality is far less superior and get less for it. The final type of dealer is a "quantity" dealer who prefers to limit his exposure to numerous customers by selling larger quantities to a select few.

Standard practices of buying and selling are constantly coming into play during all drug negotiations, with bartering and mutual compromises on each side. As in any business venture, profit margin is based on either an inflated price tag for the goods or the reduction of overhead. To help illustrate these enormous profits made in illicit drug transactions, a hypothetical shipment of cocaine will be discussed next. This is an example of a 100-kilogram shipment of cocaine from its origin in South America to its final stages of distribution on the street. This example will not only show the tremendous profit margin realized by cocaine traffickers but will also demonstrate the steps involved in manufacturing and importing the drug.

STEP 1. The cocaine manufacturing process begins when the FARMER cultivates and harvests the dry leaves of the coca plant. In this step, the leaves are refined with chemicals and solvents to create what is known as "pasta." In this stage of the manufacturing process, the farmers will use a total of 15,000 kilos (kilograms) of dried leaves to make 125 kilos of pasta which will eventually become the 100-kilo shipment.

STEP 2. Next, the pasta will be sold to the GUIDES by three to five farmers of his own nationality. The guides will then sell the pasta to a buyer, who is frequently a Colombian. The guide's job is to escort the buyer into and out of the coca cultivation area for the purchase of the pasta. The farmers' and guides' profits are a small fraction of the traffickers' once the cocaine arrives in the United States.

STEP 3. Once the BUYER has made his purchase from the guides, the pasta is then transported to a production facility known as a "base laboratory." These base labs are usually located somewhere in the Colombian countryside.

STEP 4. The BASE LABORATORIES then convert the pasta into raw cocaine base. During this process approximately 1.25 kilos of pasta are required for one kilo of base. The completed product will then be shipped to yet another location for additional processing.

STEP 5. The next phase of the production process is the CRYSTAL LAB phase. These labs are usually located in or near a major Colombian city, and it is in this process that the cocaine base is converted to its final crystal form (cocaine hydrochloride). It is here that the drug achieves its major worth, as it is considered to be anywhere from 92 percent to 98 percent pure. This also could be the stage where the initial cutting of the drug takes place.

STEP 6. The final product from several crystal labs will ultimately make up the ultimate 100-kilo shipment of cocaine. It is now the SMUGGLER who must arrange for the transportation of the cocaine from its origination city into the United States. To successfully complete this phase, the smuggler must be discreet to avoid detection and must contact as few people as possible during the importation process.

STEP 7. Once the shipment has successfully arrived in the United States, the person receiving it will be the WHOLESALER. This player will also attempt to cut the product and sell it in multiple-kilo lots to primary distributors at the point of entry.

STEP 8. The PRIMARY DISTRIBUTORS will purchase multiple-kilo lots and sell single kilos at a time. The cutting process is still continuing, so the overall quality of the original 100-kilo shipment is drastically reduced each time the drug changes hands.

STEP 9. The DEALER phase is next, but there are a number of different transactions that might take place at this point. Each purchase from this point on is considerably smaller; single kilos to pounds, pounds to half- or quarter-pounds, and quarter pounds to ounces. Each reduction in quantity experiences a significant degree of cutting.

STEP 10. The DEALER-USER will usually purchase less than one ounce at a time and will then sell gram or quarter-gram quantities to three to five customers at a time. At this pont, cutting of the drug takes place at each step. Because he uses a significant amount of his product, the dealer-user is an unreliable individual to deal with, and he usually finds himself arrested due to his own carelessness.

STEP 11. Ultimately, the CONSUMER will purchase small quantities (up to 1 gram) for alleged personal consumption. These may sell for $100 to $150 each and be of a low quality. Initially, our original 100-kilo shipment might have cost $20,000 per kilo, totaling $2,000,000 for the initial shipment, which was close to 90 percent pure. Realizing that there are 28 grams in an ounce and 16 ounces in a pound, after changing hands so many times throughout the trafficking chain, the 98,560 grams (being cut approximately 10 times) would ultimately bring approximately $98,560,000. The purity of the cocaine, by the time it reaches the street, would only be about 12 percent.

In contrast, cocaine hydrochloride purchased in South America might sell for as little as $3,000–$7,000 per pound, compared to $15,000–$25,000 per pound in the United States (Table 7).

Table 7

**Growth of Cocaine Abuse:
Estimate of Illicit Cocaine Entering
The United States in 1981 (in Tons)**

Estimated maximum illicit cocaine hydrochloride theoretically available for world use:	140	-	172
Less cocaine hydrochloride not converted because of insufficient production methods, crop loss, excessive cultivation, spoilage, loss in transit, pilferage, eradication, and seizure of prime materials:	-		90
Subtotal:	50	-	82
Less amount seized worldwide:	-		8
Subtotal:	42	-	74
Less cocaine hydrochloride exported to third countries (Europe, Canada, and Latin America):	-		12
Range of cocaine hydrochloride estimated to enter the United States market:	30	-	62

Source: Drug Enforcement Administration, Drug Enforcement, Fall 1982 (Washington D.C.: U.S. Department of Justice).

Part II

THE PLAYERS

MOTIVES, means, and money are certainly significant contributing factors to the overall illicit drug scenario. However, a basic understanding of those who personally choose this illegal occupation should also be considered. Since those involved with illicit drugs are tightly interwoven throughout society, law enforcement officers, educators, and concerned citizens alike will benefit from the understanding of who the players are and how they all fit into the total drug-trafficking scheme.

CHAPTER 5

THE NARCOTICS AGENT—A PROFILE

IN THE 1980s it is clear that specialization in any number of professions has taken precedence over generalization. We see evidence of this in such professions as medicine and law.

The field of law enforcement, though typically reluctant to accept major changes over the years, also has succumbed to this trend. However, in many smaller jurisdictions it may not be unusual for the beat patrolman to act as patrol officer, investigator, and in some instances, fire fighter. Generally speaking, in most police departments, specially trained officers work the streets in areas of both patrol and investigation.

Criminal investigation is no longer the generalized field it once was, either. Detective bureaus consist of specialists trained in the areas of homicide, arson, rape, burglary, robbery, white-collar crime, and narcotics, only to name a few.

The world has observed the work of famous homicide detectives over the decades, but only in the last twenty years or so has there been a major emphasis placed on specially trained, full-time drug investigators known as narcotics agents or, typically, "narcs."

The term "narc," as we discussed earlier, is a generic term which refers to undercover police personnel. The same term has been adopted by drug dealers and their associates to label police informers who are used by investigating agents to infiltrate drug distribution networks (see Chapter 7 on "The Informer—A Profile").

With the upsurge in illegal drug activity in the late 1950s and mid-1960s, there came an unprecedented need for police officers to learn more than ever before about drugs, their effects, prices, and street jargon in order to combat the country's growing drug problem. Officers in those early days might have worked general investigative assignments and also might have donned disguises in an effort to penetrate drug distribution operations. These specialized assignments rapidly acquired the general label of "undercover" work.

It was clearly a new era for criminal investigation in the United States and one that was largely misunderstood by the general public as well as by many members of the law enforcement community, itself. The misunderstanding of the job of narcotics investigator was primarily because the duties of an undercover investigator are usually cloaked in secrecy to safeguard the identity of the officer and the integrity of the investigation.

Today, officers in a metropolitan police department may not be qualified to be assigned to a drug investigation unit until they successfully complete anywhere from two to five years of patrol work and/or two years of general assignment in the detective bureau. Many departments, though, still employ new police recruits for undercover assignments, because their identity has not yet been known to the general public and their youthful appearance is frequently beneficial in infiltrating drug traffickers.

Many experienced officers throughout various departments find the duties of a narcotics investigator less than appealing due to the close contact drug agents must have with the criminal element, as well as the long hours and high-risk elements involved. Others, however, are intrigued by the street and the thinking processes of the criminal. They consider drug investigation as a golden opportunity to learn about the inner workings of the illicit drug business and the dangerous criminal underground.

The narcotics agent probably has one of the most active jobs in law enforcement today. This could be due to the fact that drug investigations, for the most part, are "proactive" rather than "reactive" investigations. In other words, the investigator must take to the street and generate his own case load instead of having cases assigned to him as a detective working investigations in homicide or burglary. This task is usually not that difficult, due to the tremendous influx of drug activity in most communities. The concern is just finding significant investigations worthy of the agent's time and effort.

The hours are usually long (much longer than a regularly scheduled eight-hour shift), late, and frequently require the agent's time on holidays and weekends. Depending on the assignment at hand, it is likely that agents will be called out on a moment's notice, regardless of any personal commitments.

Narcotics officers will frequently find themselves immersed in different types of investigations at one time, such as, perhaps, an air smuggling investigation, a diversion investigation, or a distribution ring that might lead to an underground laboratory. He also may find himself writing numerous search warrants every month and averaging several felony arrests per investigation, in addition to associating in an undercover capacity with intelligent high-level organized crime figures. Experience such as this is seldom acquired in less active investigative positions within many departments.

The excitement and varied pace of the job, however, is often footnoted by severe physical fatigue and sometimes intense emotional strain that may result in a disjointed personal or social life. This strain can be compounded by personal injury on the job or even injury or death of a partner and friend in the line of duty.

The narc is in a class of his own in police work, a profession with an otherwise paramilitary structure. Instead of maintaining the spit-and-polish image upheld by his fellow patrol officers, he must not only stop being seen associating with them in public but he must look, act, and dress in a fashion that will enable him to blend in with the general population and go unnoticed by alert drug dealers.

In the case of long-term undercover assignments, the officer may be required to assume a completely new identity while associating with suspected drug dealers. This type of investigation is often viewed as a subterfuge and possibly, in the eyes of radical and uninformed defense attorneys, as grounds for an entrapment defense. In reality, however, the role of an undercover police officer is a legal, inventive, and highly effective form of criminal investigation that has long been recognized and sanctioned by the United States Supreme Court.

THE JOB

The law enforcement community, in general, strives to constantly update and maintain standards of training and education of its police personnel. Officers are continually required to attend in-service training throughout the year to help them keep abreast of any changes in investigative technique, criminal law, or any other facet of their job. It is becoming more and more evident that in the business of drug law enforcement, there is an increasing need for additional training to keep up with ever-changing street prices, terminology, drug identification, and investigative technique.

Nowadays, the candidates for narcotic agent will probably be required to have a bachelor's degree in some field and, in some cases, a significant police background. This is particularly true of most state police agencies and federal law enforcement agencies that enforce drug laws.

Agent training usually begins with the basic police academy. State laws usually require completion of the program and certification within the first year of employment. An intensive drug training school should follow sometime before the end of the first year on the job. The drug investigation schools are technical training schools throughout the United States (for certified officers only) and are usually sponsored by the U.S. government, state police agencies, or certified training facilities. New agents will then continue training as they work and get promoted as their job performance dictates, just as in any police position.

The problems of job-related stress begin as the agents realize that there are more investigations to go around than investigators to work them. This scenario then finds agents working a fifty- to sixty-hour week in an effort to satisfy the demands of police administrators. These frustrations manifest themselves in big city police departments that have ample manpower but little money appropriated to purchase drugs with. Conversely, state police agencies seem to have little problem in acquiring funds to purchase drugs, sometimes ranging from $100,000 to $200,000 per year, but often experience severe manpower shortages.

Due to the transient nature of the drug trafficker, all law enforcement agencies should work closely together, exchanging information and pooling resources, to reduce the overall work load. This, however, is not always the case due to petty political jealousies and inter-agency competition for case recognition.

The day-to-day activities of the narcotics agent could be described as both boring and dangerous at the same time. While involved routinely with interviews, lengthy surveillances, and mountains of paperwork, agents are frequently faced with situations that place them in immediate fear for their life. These situations usually involve either working undercover, conducting surveillance, or effecting arrests.

Although working in an undercover capacity is considered one of the most intriguing and gratifying aspects of the job, it also poses some unique dangers and problems (see Chapter 10 on "Fundamentals of Drug Investigation").

THE STRESS

A career as a narcotics investigator, as already indicated, may have considerable stress-related consequences. As always, the severity of stress on any job will vary greatly from individual to individual. There are many causes and effects of stress, as well as many possible ways to alleviate it.

Any number of stimuli contribute to the stress-related problems experienced by narcotics officers. Initially, the job of drug enforcement poses all of the stressful aspects of general police work, such as:

- Hostility from the public
- Fear of death or bodily harm
- Administrative pressure from supervisors/administrators
- Little or no acknowledgement for a job well done
- Changes in agency policy/procedure

In addition to the above factors, stressing factors commonly experienced by drug enforcement officers in particular are:

- Long and unscheduled hours
- Hazardous undercover duty
- In some cases, no overtime pay
- Erratic and unbalanced eating habits
- Extended exposure to adverse weather
- Frequent weekend or holiday overtime

Numerous occupations, including many medical-related jobs and high-level corporate positions, for example, have been associated with a high stress variable, as well as the job of drug enforcement. Stress may very well result in a loss of efficiency as well as increased physical and emotional problems. These problems may account for the high rate of suicide and divorce that traditionally prevails within such professions.

As mentioned, physical problems may result from a stressful working environment and may later manifest themselves as heart ailments, gastrointestinal malfunctions, and skin disorders, to name a few. Additionally, emotional strain may result in severe nervous conditions or various forms of neurosis, which may result in an unbalanced personal and social life.

Often, these conditions create a domino-type effect on the worker. This means that the more problems one has, the more stress he is under, and vice versa.

It is recommended that police agencies assigning officers to enforce drug violations implement an in-house program to evaluate the physical, mental and emotional condition of their drug enforcement personnel. These evaluations may be conducted throughout any phase of an agent's tour of duty and may provide police administrators insight into any problems that might ultimately jeopardize the agent's physical or mental health. In addition, early detection of physical or emotional strain might avoid the compromising of any ongoing investigations.

Finally, a source of stress unique to undercover personnel is the constant association with the criminal element. Due to hazardous undercover duty, in particular long-term "deep-cover" assignments, agents are constantly subjected to individuals whose life-styles might differ greatly from that of the agent. In some instances agents regularly observe criminal behavior and activities that might prove to be morally offensive. During these undercover situations, it is common for suspects to offer drugs to the agents, hoping to be assured that the agent is also a drug user and not a policeman. This creates much stress for the agent in both his professional and personal affairs.

CHAPTER 6

THE DRUG DEALER—A PROFILE

SHODDY CLOTHING or jailhouse tattoos are no longer the sterotypic trademarks of drug dealers. Today's drug criminal is not limited to any particular business or social status; indeed, he could be anyone.

The term "drug dealer," like so many terms in this business, is a general term referring to any of several plateaus of distribution within the trafficking chain. Anyone, from the time a drug is being processed to the time that it is sold in its smallest quantities on the street, could be referred to as a "drug dealer." Police, on the other hand, have traditionally adopted their own "in-house" slang for the drug dealer, which is considered by some to be less than tactful. In an effort to maintain a professional decorum throughout this text, we will simply call them "suspects."

The FBI reports an estimated half million drug dealers are arrested each year, but that figure is most likely a gross understatement. The actual figure, including federal, state, and local arrests, is probably much higher, since the huge revenues from illegal drug activity have substantially surpassed the revenues of many major U.S. industries. In 1980, for example, illegal drug traffic was estimated at $79 billion in retail sales volume. This is considerably larger than the profits realized in the computer or clothing markets.

According to the U.S. Department of Justice, Bureau of Justice Statistics, a composite portrait of a typical drug law offender shows a white male about thirty years old. Because drug offenses encompass widely differing types of drug acts, violators may be white-collar employees, unemployed drug addicts, street corner dealers, or successful businessmen. Persons charged with drug possession seem to be younger than those charged with the sale of drugs, and the manufacturers seem to be the oldest of all.

Over the years, law enforcement has documented a significant increase in the number of criminals choosing a career in illicit drug traffic. For instance, the number of drug law violators convicted in federal district courts rose from 1,400 in 1964 to 6,300 in 1982.

Ironically, with the growing number of criminals involved in drug law violations, it is increasingly difficult to predict whether a drug dealer will be apprehended. The Bureau of Justice Statistics, however, has estimated that once caught, the conviction rate for these criminals is about 76 percent. The bad news is that, on the average, about 85 percent of those who are convicted only serve about five years or less.

LEVELS OF DISTRIBUTION

The different terms for "dealer" that people typically hear on the street or read in the newspaper are discussed next.

THE MANUFACTURER. This is a term given to those who literally manufacture drugs such as cocaine, heroin, or methamphetamine from the raw base product. These individuals possess the "know-how" to mix specific chemicals together to produce the finished marketable product. Some manufacturers even have a background in biochemistry to aid them in their work.

While street cocaine and heroin are drugs that are primarily manufactured in foreign countries, amphetamine and methamphetamine are, for the most part, manufactured in underground or "clandestine" laboratories in the United States.

THE IMPORTER. This is the individual who frequently works with the smuggler devising a scheme in which to introduce the drug into other countries for distribution (this also applies to exporters). The importer frequently has a significant financial investment in the product and, while associating with high-level traffickers, often realizes vast profits from its sales.

THE TRAFFICKER/PRIMARY DISTRIBUTOR. This group disburses the finished product over a broad geographical area once it has reached its port of entry. If the drug were methamphetamine, manufactured in Little Rock, Arkansas, for example, the trafficker would dispatch it to other areas within the state and possibly to other states where trafficking associates had been established. The same distribution pattern is true for drugs brought into the country by smugglers.

THE SMUGGLER. For the most part, he is the one who physically transports the drug from its place of origin to its initial destination. Although the activities of the smuggler and the trafficker are distinct, one individual might perform both functions. The smuggler may use any of several methods of transportation to accomplish this task (see Chapter 12 on "Smuggling Activities"). In the case of an air smuggler, for example, it is his job to determine the safest route to travel in order to avoid detection by law enforcement authorities. His job may also require him to make arrangements with a ground crew who will assist him in offloading his payload once it arrives at its destination. The smuggler's methods of operation vary and are limited only by his imagination and resources.

THE DISTRIBUTOR. Multi-pound lots of drugs such as cocaine, heroin, or marijuana are dealt in by this person. It is likely that there are distributors in every major city in the United States who receive huge shipments of drugs for resale on a regular basis. They may be people who have legitimate jobs as a "front" for their illegal activities such as a banker, attorney, etc. These violators are usually well known to the local drug enforcement authorities and have long-standing and trusted associates who are also involved with the local drug trade.

THE DEALER. This usually refers to the person who is capable of selling multi-ounces of product. Remember that an ounce of cocaine, for example, sells for an average of $2,000. This individual has a much higher visibility on the street to potential drug buyers. In other words, he makes his presence known to a much broader audience, many of whom do not know him on a personal basis but are willing to trust him because of his street reputation as a dealer. This higher profile, of course, makes him a much easier target for detection by law enforcement authorities.

THE DEALER-USER. He is the small-time seller who is usually his own worst enemy. This is true by virtue of the fact that his ability to sell discreetly is often hampered by his own craving for the drug he is selling. This can result in his making bad deals for a poor-quality product at a high price. Often, he will show poor judgment in selecting his buyers, because he is "high" on his own product or just being careless. Violators who fall into this category are often good candidates for informers AFTER they are arrested, because of their direct association with larger-scale dealers, as well as their status as repeat offenders who will probably be facing a jail sentence.

THE CONSUMER. This is the individual who claims that he is just a recreational user. Even though this claim is frequently made, this recreational user usually finds himself locating drugs for friends and selling small quantities or "giving" (distributing) quantities of drugs to associates. The law, of course, does not differentiate between friends and strangers, so the act is usually considered distribution and deemed a serious felony.

Society can thank the drug consumer for nurturing a perpetual marketplace for drugs and providing a never-ending financial incentive for established and aspiring drug dealers in every level of the drug-selling hierarchy.

STRINGERS

Drug dealers on almost any level of the echelon will attempt to use other persons or "stringers" to accomplish their goals. These stringers participate for varying reasons, but, for the most part, they are not the "Brains" behind any distribution scheme and have limited knowledge of the overall operation. They are, however, often handsomely compensated for their assistance with money, drugs, weapons or other commodities.

Let's now look at a few of the most common "stringers" associated with the drug business.

THE MULE. This is a term typically used to describe a low-level stringer who is willing to transport drugs for short-term profits. The mule may do this in a variety of different ways as the following hypothetical examples illustrate:

1. A female transporting a kilo (kilogram) of cocaine which is strapped to her stomach area might give the outward appearance of being pregnant.
2. A weary college student flying home for the holidays could be "body packing" sixteen one-ounce packets of heroin that are individually taped to his arms and legs and concealed by winter clothing.
3. A work-release inmate at a state penitentiary may swallow three to five balloons of heroin just before he returns to the institution, only to regurgitate them and give them to a dealer behind the walls for distribution.

The mule plays an integral part in the drug-distribution process since he serves as a buffer between law enforcement authorities and the dealers themselves. Often, narcotics agents will apprehend the mule but be unable to collect enough evidence on his employer to make an arrest. In this case, the criminal justice system will have to settle for the mule only, who will be prosecuted as diligently as the distributor himself.

In such instances the mule might "turn state's evidence" as a police informer and provide narcotics agents with assistance in drug investigations. This assistance may be in exchange for prosecutorial immunity on pending charges against the mule (see Chapter 7, "The Informer—A Profile").

COUNTERSURVEILLANCE. In almost any criminal organization, some people on the fringe of the operation are willing to offer protective or informative services for the criminals running the organization. This is certainly also true for many drug distribution networks. This type of individual performs his task by overseeing big money drug deals in a countersurveillance capacity. His job can be to accomplish any of the following functions:

1. Intelligence function: to inform the dealers of police-type personnel in the area of an ongoing drug transaction.
2. Tactical function I: to act as an armed bodyguard to prevent associates in a transaction from stealing ("ripping off") the drugs or money.
3. Tactical function II: to aid the dealer in an escape from police during a drug "bust" (arrest situation).

Those involved in countersurveillance are usually compensated with drugs by the drug dealer who employs them. They may, however, be paid in cash, stolen merchandise or any other suitable commodity agreed upon.

Once police have identified countersurveillance personnel during a drug transaction, those who participate are also arrested along with the dealers and usually are charged with aiding and abetting, conspiracy to distribute, or any other applicable violation of the drug laws.

A CRIMINAL PROFILE

One of the first things any police officer learns is that when dealing with people and the unpredictable human nature factor, the unexpected can usually be expected. Somewhat contrary to this basic philosophy is the fact that many criminals over the decades have managed to establish a profile that can be easily identified by the narcotics investigator. This profile repeats itself again and again throughout different investigations and may aid the investigator in predicting the next move of his target (Table 8).

Table 8

Defendant Characteristics: Manufacturers, Dealers, Possessors

	Manuf.	Deal.	Poss.	All Drug Offenders
Less than 26 years old	19%	26%	39%	27%
No college education	70%	76%	76%	75%
Unmarried	60%	67%	72%	66%
No dependents	38%	39%	51%	41%
Income $10,000 or less	74%	78%	81%	78%
Prior record	51%	53%	33%	49%

Source: U.S. Department of Justice, National Institute of Justice, Bureau of Justice Statistics Bulletin; Federal Drug Law Violators, p. 2.

An examination of a few of these criminal "types" might indicate to what degree a criminal is involved in what type of crime.

THE OCCASIONAL CRIMINAL. As the name implies, this individual is involved in criminal activity on an erratic basis. He may not have the know-how or contacts to commit crimes regularly enough to make a living but, given the right chance at the right time, will not hesitate to involve himself in felonious activity.

While this individual may have a legitimate job, he associates regularly with others more actively involved in criminal activity. These associates provide the occasional criminal his random opportunities.

THE OPPORTUNIST. The opportunist acts, for the most part, on the spur of the moment without much forethought. This criminal is often involved in several types of crimes at once, ranging from drug dealing to burglary to robbery. Since he is most concerned with making a "quick buck" and since he is not a "career" criminal, his mode of operation will often be sloppy.

THE PROFESSIONAL/CAREER CRIMINAL. Illegal activity is the primary manner in which this individual makes a living. Usually with a lengthy criminal history and friends who have also spent time in the penitentiary, the professional criminal is not interested in legitimate gainful employment. He usually is good at what he does and, because of long established criminal contacts, may successfully avoid detection by police authorities for long periods of time.

THE HABITUAL CRIMINAL. This type of criminal usually possesses a lengthy criminal history that is indicative of his contempt for the law. This criminal type still strives for new ways to break the law and dabbles in an array of illegal occupations.

Many states have enacted habitual violator laws to keep this kind of individual from returning to the streets. For the habitual criminal, an occasional brief sentence in the penitentiary is usually not a sufficient deterrent for future involvement in crime.

Society should note that the ignorant or novice criminal will not always stay that way "bust" after "bust." Each time a violator is apprehended and taken through the criminal justice system, he experiences an ongoing education by virtue of the proceedings he is subjected to during adjudication.

Unfortunately, if he is halfway attentive he will learn many weaknesses of police investigations, interrogations, search-and-seizure laws and any other aspect of the criminal justice process which might benefit him later in his criminal endeavors.

CHAPTER 7

THE INFORMER—A PROFILE

THROUGHOUT the course of any criminal investigation, the investigator must recognize his most valuable investigative tools and become familiar with them as best as possible. Second only to the policeman's revolver, the informer could be the most powerful tool the law enforcement profession can use against the criminal element in general.

From those involved in high-level organized crime, to corporate wheeling and dealing, to even everyday office politics, the informer rears his ugly head and makes his presence known to even the most powerful of individuals.

Remember a little incident known as "Watergate"? It was then presidential legal advisor, John Dean, who came forth to "tell all" to the public in one of the most widely publicized political scandals in American history.

Joe Valachi was a one-time trusted member of the Mafia's rank and file until federal authorities convinced him to turn federal witness against his associates in 1963.

The list goes on and on. The real danger or benefit of the informer depends on whether you are the informer or the target of the informer.

To further understand just why anyone would choose to become an informer, one must first study and understand a few of the underlying psychological motivations involved. The most common profiles are described as follows:

MOTIVATIONS

The Fear Motive

Probably the most productive informer is one motivated by fear, at least from a criminal investigation standpoint. This type of informer is afraid, for one reason or another, for his own well-being, for a family member, or for an associate.

The informer's fear-motive is a kind of self-inflicted fear that can result from a variety of circumstances. One of the most common fears is that of going to jail after being arrested on a felony violation, in particular if he is a repeat offender.

After an arrest is made, the suspect may be granted an interview with investigators. If the police feel that the suspect is acquainted with another criminal higher up the ladder, then the suspect may be given the opportunity to become an informer.

If the suspect agrees to this arrangement, he will usually do so after being assured that he will be facing fewer criminal charges or a lesser sentence in exchange for his services. Generally, the police do not have the authority to grant such a condition; however, the prosecutor may authorize it at his discretion.

An informant working under these conditions is termed a "hammered" informant, and from this point on, as the informant works with the investigator, he realizes that if he fails to produce the necessary information or services, the original deal will be off. He can then expect to be prosecuted as originally charged.

Often, an informer in the above predicament will work off his charges as agreed upon and continue to work with the police on other cases. This usually happens when the informer and his control agent establish a bond of trust between each other, resulting in a successful working relationship.

The Perverse Motivation

Dealing with cunning and intelligent criminals makes the investigator realize that his adversary may resort to some of the same undercover techniques as the police. Evidence of this can be found in the informer with perverse motivations. This is the informer who is "up to something," or one whose seemingly innocent motives cloak a hidden objective.

This type of informant will usually approach the police on his own and offer informative services, claiming legitimate motives. These alleged motives may be any of the following:

1. Realizing the dangers of drug abuse and wanting to assist the police.
2. Becoming religious and claiming that drugs are the work of the devil.

3. Needing extra money.
4. Claiming to be a former addict and wanting to turn in pushers.

Even though all potential informers should be considered for use, it is the responsibility of the investigator to decipher the true motives of his operatives. This kind of informer may very well be the most dangerous informer that the police have to deal with for several reasons which are outlined below:

1. He may want a chance to come to police headquarters to see what the undercover officers look like so he can either identify them in his own drug-dealing activities, or pass on physical descriptions and names of undercover personnel to his associates.
2. Through the course of the initial interview, he may ask for the names of drug dealers currently under investigation by the department in order to offer assistance in making cases on them. If the officer succumbs to this infiltrating technique, then he is conveying more information to the criminal than the criminal is to the officer. Friends of drug dealers often use this technique to report to their associates as to how close the police are to their own operations.
3. The potential informer may approach the officer with an offer of assistance and promise numerous big-name dealers in the area. This individual may, however, request some expense money before he actually does any work. If the officer pays the informer at this point, he may never see him again, or the informer may continue to return for more expense money time and time again without offering any valuable or workable information. This is why investigators must require informers to "produce" before any payments have been made.

The Mercenary Motive

This informer works for money and, for the most part, will provide information on almost anyone for the right price. This is the guy who will call his control agent day and night with all kinds of reasons for needing more money, and all kinds of reasons for spending what has just been given him the day before.

Investigators must be careful when using informers with this motive, since payments on a case-by-case basis may be looked upon by courts as a basis for entrapment. That is, the informer, if low on money, may theoretically "set up" someone just so he can acquire more money. This is why it is a good idea for the investigator to always document conversations between drug suspects and informers before any transactions occur to establish the suspect's criminal intent.

The purchasing of information is not a bad practice, as many criminals can be successfully motivated by periodic payments. For the most part, it is this money motivation that attracts persons to criminal activity anyway, which can be used successfully to the advantage of the police.

It should be noted, however, that the mercenary motive is frequently coupled with the motive of revenge against associates and is also a strong incentive when coupled with any of the other motives.

The Revenge Motive

Revenge is a motive that has spurred many a violent act within the criminal underground. This is not an uncommon motive for any potential informative source, but as stated above, the investigator must have the ability to spot this motive, as it could place him in great danger later on in the investigation.

The types of revenge differ, but some examples are listed as follows:

1. A petty criminal who feels that he is being treated unfairly by his associates and wanting a bigger piece of the pie.
2. A jealous girl friend, boy friend, wife or husband wanting to "get even."
3. A dealer who is also a chronic user of drugs and has become careless in his dealing. Suppliers may recognize this and "cut off" the dealer from the drugs and try to locate other more reliable associates. The user may then inform on the supplier for revenge.

The Egotistical Motive (The Dick Tracy Syndrome)

This motive, as the nickname implies, is an unusual motivation associated with both criminals and those who are considered police fans. This individual tends to magnify his own importance by associating with police officers and rendering bits of information about criminal activities. It seems strange that a civilian would want to involve himself with a dangerous criminal element just for the sake of associating with policemen, but it does happen. It is not always the law-abiding citizen who falls into this category but often criminals wishing to curry the favor of the officers to be well thought of by the law enforcement community.

This informer can be a highly effective criminal source and is worthy of consideration by criminal investigators.

The Unwitting Informer

Although working undercover can produce many hazards for the undercover agent, there are many discrete advantages. One advantage is the ability for the agent to be in a situation where he can systematically develop criminal sources who may provide the agent information without realizing it. This source is termed an "unwitting informer."

The development of this kind of source simply involves befriending a drug dealer, user, or even an associate who is well aquainted with numerous individuals in the drug business. Small acts of generosity such as buying a drink or offering a ride may pave the way to a relationship where the informer may introduce the agent to dealers for drug purchases.

Depending on the degree of involvement of the unwitting informer, he could also be charged as an accomplice to drug sales in which they are involved. This can happen when the dealer gives the informer money, drugs or other compensation for his role in the introduction.

Regardless of which informant profile is identified, investigators must always look on their informer with caution. An informer who appears to be a policeman's friend one day may turn on him the next, resulting in compromised investigations and, possibly, damaged police careers.

A bond of friendship must be established, however, between the informer and his control agent in any successful investigation. The investigator must constantly keep this bond under control to keep the informant from learning more than necessary about the investigation, the agent, or his personal affairs.

Under no circumstances should an informer learn the address of the control agent or other agent personnel. Additionally, the officer must be careful not to inadvertently mention the names of his or her spouse and children or places where they work or attend school.

Special caution must be exerted when working with informers who are the opposite sex of their control agents. When possible, agents should be accompanied by partners when meeting the informer, in case there are allegations later on of professional misconduct on the part of the interviewing officer (see the section "Working Informants" in Chapter 10, "Fundamentals of Drug Investigation").

Part III

DRUG ENFORCEMENT

HOW ARE the activities of a secret illegal enterprise uncovered and destroyed? In order for the drug trafficker to be detected, law enforcement must not only learn the drug business as thoroughly as its illegal counterpart but have the knowledge and ability to detect, apprehend, and convict these criminals.

Criminals and narcotics agents alike operate on different levels, depending on who they work for and what resources are available to them. These resources may include manpower, money, electronic gadgetry, and know-how.

SEARCH AND SEIZURE
EVIDENCE

CHAPTER 8

THE DRUG LAWS – THE NARC'S TOOLBOX

INTRODUCTION

JUST AS the gun aids the police officer in his duties, knowledge of the law can be one of the most powerful tools afforded to the narcotics investigator. The comprehension and understanding of criminal law is considered to be one of the more tedious aspects of police job training, and much of what is taught is frequently lost due to dry subject matter and an overall lack of interest.

Criminal law is dynamic, as it is not just a set of fixed principles but also the judicial branch's ongoing interpretation of them. Today's professional police officer realizes that understanding and retaining state and federal law, in addition to recent Supreme Court decisions, will make his job much easier. The problems associated with learning law are that it changes so frequently and that what was law ten years ago may not necessarily be law today. Consequently, officers must work through regularly scheduled in-service training to keep up with the times.

As indicated above, changes in the law that do occur are twofold. First, the changes in state and federal legislation comprise the state and federal laws, respectively. These must be noted by every law enforcement agency so changes in policy and procedure can be adopted accordingly. Secondly, there is the issue of Supreme Court decisions or "judge made law." Supreme Court decisions are made on both the state and federal level and, for the most part, decide controversial or questionable issues regarding criminal cases previously tried by lower courts.

When a criminal appeals a conviction obtained in a trial court, a district court, appeals court, and/or the state supreme court will review the evidence in the case. The court will then decide if it should affirm the original conviction or overturn (reverse) it. The same procedure takes place when a state supreme court decision is appealed and the U.S. Supreme Court makes the ultimate determination. This process is a long one due to the tremendous backlog of cases. The wait could be as long as two years. During this period, it is likely that the convicted criminal might be released from jail on an appeal bond and be free to continue his criminal activities.

These appellate decisions are, in effect, law and not only serve as rules that the police must observe in their everyday duties but can also play a large part in the formulation of police agency policy and procedure.

This chapter is designed not to make criminal law experts out of its readers but to acquaint the reader with a few significant and recent laws that might benefit narcotics agents in the peformance of their duties.

DISTRIBUTION

Generally, since the passing of the Uniform Controlled Substances Act in 1970, most states have enacted their own laws dealing with illegal distribution or delivery of controlled substances. When charging a suspected drug dealer with the crime of distribution or delivery, it is incumbent on the part of the state to show the defendant's "criminal intent." For the most part, this is not too difficult when dealing with a hand-to-hand sale of drugs from the suspect to an undercover police officer. In this instance, voice recordings, photographs, video recordings, and the testimony of police witnesses are used to prove the case in court. Conversations between an undercover agent (or informant) and the drug dealer might also strengthen distribution cases in which a dealer employs a girl friend or other accomplice as a middleman to sell the drugs to an agent while insulating himself from the police. The conversations before, during, and after the transaction, if documented properly, may be suitable as evidence to prove the criminal intent of the primary dealer as well as his accomplices for charges of distribution.

This case often involves associates who are not dealers themselves but are people working for drug dealers by either introducing the buyer to the seller, loaning vehicles to the seller for transportation to or from the deal, or possibly providing the seller the use of a residence for the purposes of completing the drug transaction. In these instances, the accomplices should be charged with complicity in the offense, providing their knowledge of the transaction can be shown in court. This can be done by documenting an accomplice receiving drugs, money, or any other type of compensation for their involvement in the transaction or by recording an undercover statement made by the accomplice implicating his/her involvement in the offense.

POSSESSION WITH INTENT TO DISTRIBUTE

Another commonly used law in drug enforcement is that of possession with intent to distribute controlled substances or felony possession. The elements which comprise this charge may vary greatly from state to state, but the criminal intent variable still applies. It is important for police officers to understand the differences between "simple possession" and "possession with intent to distribute." Knowing the different elements of each type of offense can be the difference between a misdemeanor or a felony charge and will play a significant role in the amount of time the defendant serves if convicted.

Generally, the manner in which drugs are packaged will be a good indicator as to the suspect's intent to distribute. As an example, if a search warrant is served on a residence and twenty-eight gram packets of cocaine are discovered, it should be obvious that the method of packaging is not for personal consumption but for distribution to various buyers. Furthermore, the quantity of drugs seized may also provide the police with sufficient reason to believe possession with intent is the proper charge rather than simple possession. Another example would be if a kilogram (2.2 lbs.) of marijuana were seized, it would most likely constitute possession with intent to distribute as opposed to misdemeanor possession.

Other factors that may help prove possession with intent to distribute could be seizing paraphernalia located near the drugs, such as scales; numerous empty, clear plastic bags commonly used for packaging powders and marijuana; address books indicating drug customers and amounts owed or received; unused bindles commonly used for packaging gram quantities of powders; and finally, large sums of money located in close proximity to drugs (see Chapter 2, "Drug Familiarization").

SIMPLE POSSESSION

For the most part, simple possession is considered to be misdemeanor possession of drugs. As earlier mentioned, these laws vary from state to state, but many of the elements are universal. With the exception of jurisdictions where laws set forth a specified amount of drugs that constitute simple possession, great discretion must be used when determining the difference between simple possession and possession with intent to distribute.

Many times a simple possession charge is the most serious charge that can be filed against a drug suspect. Investigating officers, however, have the responsibility of determining any previous convictions of the drug suspect to better determine what charge should be filed. A previous felony conviction, for instance, may be justification for the filing of felony charges against the accused rather than a simple misdemeanor. This criteria may require the previous conviction to be that of a drug conviction, but the law could consider any felony conviction grounds for the filing of a felony charge.

In almost every jurisdiction, the prosecution must prove actual or constructive possession of the controlled substance together with the knowledge of the presence and character of the substance. In other words, it must be proven that the suspect was intentionally and consciously in possession of the drugs.

FORFEITURE LAWS

One of the more powerful legal tools afforded to law enforcement in their fight against illicit drugs is the ability to seize personal assets of the drug trafficker. The law provides the police this ability through forfeiture provisions designed to hit the drug dealer where it may hurt most (in his wallet) and create a deterrent for would-be drug dealers. The existence of these laws is nothing new, but the extensive use of them is a relatively new tactic used more and more by drug enforcement agents and prosecutors alike. The 1984 Comprehensive Crime Act increased existing federal forfeiture powers, while most states have passed individual legislation addressing their own forfeiture needs.

On the federal level, prosecutors have used forfeiture laws quite successfully in several recent major cases. In 1983, for example, more than $100 million in cash and property was seized and forfeited to the government by convicted criminals. To seize property for forfeiture, the government must show that the property was acquired through illegal drug revenues or was used to facilitate the dealing of drugs. Cash found as a result of a search warrant may be seized, provided it was located in close proximity to illegal drugs.

It is important to note here that "innocent" third parties who have a possessory interest in the seized property may intervene in the proceedings and block forfeiture.

In the 1980s it is not uncommon for drug enforcement agents to seize cars, trucks, airplanes, real estate, foreign and domestic bank accounts, or anything else deemed seizable through these innovative and powerful laws.

CONSPIRACY LAWS

The use of undercover agents and police informants is a proven asset to drug enforcement efforts all over the world. The effectiveness of undercover operatives, however, often diminish the further up the ladder they go. Many investigations prohibit the use of an undercover agent at all, because the target subject may be too heavily insulated by associates or the suspect might be considered too dangerous. It is here that a conspiracy investigation should be considered.

Federal law, as well as most state laws, possess conspiracy statutes that are widely used by law enforcement officers in the drug-suppression effort. A conspiracy is technically defined as an agreement between two or more persons to violate the law, accompanied by an overt act to further the agreement. According to law, and under the definition of conspiracy, the crime itself does not have to be completed by the perpetrators. By using this law, drug suspects do not have to be caught in possession of drugs in order to be charged with conspiracy to distribute.

To cite a simplified example, suspect "A" meets with suspect "B" and agrees to pay him $40,000 for a kilo of cocaine. Suspect "B" agrees to deliver the cocaine to a specified location on the following Tuesday. Suspect "A' answers that he will pay for the cocaine in $100 bills, which will be contained in a black briefcase. When Tuesday arrives, drug agents observe suspect "A" go to the bank and withdraw $40,000 in $100 bills and place the currency in a black briefcase. Agents may now arrest both suspects and charge them with conspiracy to violate the Controlled Substances Act. In the preceding scenario, agents should document the initial agreement between the suspects, as well as observe the overt act, to make a sound conspiracy case.

According to Howard Abadinsky in his book entitled *Organized Crime,* conspiracies may be made in three ways: the "wheel conspiracy," the "chain conspiracy," and the "enterprise conspiracy." Respectively, the wheel conspiracy is made by first identifying one main suspect as the "hub," who conspires with two or more additional suspects who are called the "spokes." In this type of conspiracy all members of the conspiracy must be aware of each other and agree on one common goal, which is termed the "rim."

Chain conspiracies are considered much easier to investigate than wheel conspiracies. In a chain conspiracy, the members of the conspiracy realize that the success of a particular criminal act is dependent on each member of the chain. These cases are easiest to make when there is only one crime being plotted, such as drug trafficking.

When more than one crime is planned, an enterprise conspiracy might be considered. In an enterprise conspiracy, all that needs to be shown is each suspect's agreement to join the criminal organization (the enterprise) by committing two or more acts of racketeering. In this type of conspiracy, members may not be aware of each other's involvement, and they may be working toward several different criminal goals at once.

WIRETAPS

The use of wiretaps by law enforcement authorities has been considered one of the more effective tools used in drug suppression. Although not as widely used as many people think, the wiretap has aided prosecutors in countless convictions of high-volume drug traffickers. Some individual states have their own wiretap legislation, while others do not. The federal wiretap law, also known as "Title III," is a comprehensive law that is constantly used by federal law enforcement agencies such as the FBI and DEA.

A wiretap, simply put, is a tool to aid officers in putting together a conspiracy investigation. Wiretaps are extremely difficult to obtain and highly scrutinized by prosecutors and judges, because they permit officers to eavesdrop on conversations between two persons who otherwise have what the law terms a "reasonable expectation of privacy."

Federal law and procedure mandate that all investigative leads must have been exhausted before the issuance of a court order by a judge will be considered. These leads must be fully documented by investigators and included in the application for the wire (called the affidavit). This document may be so inundated with details that it could easily be over

100 pages long and take months to collect sufficient data. The procedure of administrating a wiretap is time consuming and demanding, requiring special equipment and expertise and a generous complement of officers to run the equipment and provide mobile surveillance. Because of this, many police agencies elect to forgo the ordeal of trying for a wiretap unless the case involves a major, high-level criminal figure worthy of such a commitment.

Once a court order for a wiretap has been signed, law enforcement officers are duty bound to maintain the wire pursuant to the order. Court orders may require officers to conduct the wire for up to thirty days. If no evidence has been obtained during that period of time, the wire must be terminated. If evidence of ongoing criminal activity is documented, however, an extension will most likely be granted by the judge for an additional thirty days.

The most attractive benefit of a wiretap is that recorded conversations of criminal involvement are considered the best evidence and usually result in massive guilty pleas by those accused.

R.I.C.O.

The Racketeer Influenced and Corrupt Organizations (R.I.C.O.) statute has been widely used by drug enforcement officials across the country in recent history. The law, however, has been on the books since 1970 and is considered to be one of the most powerful legal tools that law enforcement possesses in the 1980s. To charge a suspect under R.I.C.O., the law requires a "pattern of racketeering" must be established and may include any of the following offenses:

1. Narcotics violations
2. Sports bribery
3. Bribery
4. Obstruction of justice
5. Counterfeiting
6. Bankruptcy fraud

The four main provisions of R.I.C.O. are simplified and itemized below:

1. It is unlawful for anyone to receive money that was acquired through a pattern of racketeering and invest it in any establishment, operation, or enterprise which is engaged in interstate or foreign commerce.

2. It is unlawful for any person through a pattern of racketeering to acquire or maintain control of any enterprise that is involved in interstate or foreign commerce.
3. It is unlawful for anyone employed or associated with enterprises involving interstate or foreign commerce to conduct affairs involving a pattern of racketeering or the collection of an unlawful debt through the enterprise.
4. It is unlawful for any person to conspire to violate any of items 1, 2, or 3.

This law has proven effective in the successful prosecution of high-level organized crime figures throughout the country. Once convicted of R.I.C.O., a defendant may be fined up to $25,000 and/or may receive up to twenty years in the penitentiary.

The unfortunate aspect of R.I.C.O. is that it fails to adequately define the terms "racketeering" and "organized crime," making it easily abused by private attorneys wishing to apply the civil provisions of the law to an ordinary business context. In addition, prosecuting attorneys have attempted to use R.I.C.O. against criminals that have virtually no ties to organized crime activities, resulting in many defendants not being sent to prison because judges feel that the R.I.C.O. penalties are too severe for low-level criminals.

SUPREME COURT DECISIONS

Search and Seizure

The subject of search and seizure is a perpetual topic of training with any police agency. It is this area that is probably undergoing change more often than any other area of law. As previously mentioned, many Supreme Court decisions are made in favor of the criminal, but, conversely, many also afford the police officer more latitude with which to conduct methods of search and seizure. Itemized next are a few of the more beneficial laws regarding search and seizure.

The Carroll Doctrine

In recent years the Carroll Doctrine has clarified the complex issues of automobile searches by further defining and broadening basic, long-standing stop-and-frisk philosophies. Basically, this decision enables police officers to search an automobile without a search warrant under the proper set of circumstances.

It is based on the theory that if officers suspect a vehicle of containing contraband or other evidence and they subsequently attempt to acquire a warrant, the vehicle may be gone when the officers return. Carroll allows a spontaneous search of the vehicle, including the passenger area, glove box, trunk, and even containers within the vehicle, provided probable cause exists that evidence of a particular crime is contained in the area of the vehicle searched.

Authorization for the searching of vehicles has even been expanded since the Carroll Doctrine in *Florida* v. *Meyers* (1984). This decision states that vehicles that have been impounded by police may still be searched and secured in an impound lot. In these decisions, the Supreme Court has determined that a person does not have the same right to privacy in a motor vehicle as he does in his own home.

Plain View

This is another area of search and seizure which the Supreme Court has ruled in favor of the policeman. The plain view ruling merely states that evidence may be seized without a warrant provided the following three criteria exists:

1. The police officer must be in a place where he has a legal right to be.
2. It must be immediately apparent that the item seized is contraband, is evidence of a crime, or otherwise offends against the law.
3. Whatever is seized must have been found "inadvertently."

This valuable ruling can be used by both drug enforcement personnel and beat patrolmen. It is important to remember here that once an item in plain view has been seized, officers do not have the legal right to proceed to search the rest of the premises without a warrant. The initial seizure, however, will most likely be sufficient grounds for acquiring a search warrant.

CHAPTER 9

THE ROLES OF DRUG ENFORCEMENT

IN TODAY'S drug-oriented society, it is likely that the average police officer knows more about drugs than did his counterpart fifteen years ago. Furthermore, the overall resources afforded to law enforcement agencies are much greater today than ever before in history. Numerous agencies throughout the United States have the authority to investigate drug law violations. These law enforcement agencies each fall under a particular level of government that dictates the extent of their jurisdiction. These are divided into three "primary" levels of government: federal, state, and local jurisdictions. Some agencies have varying responsibilities in law enforcement in general, while others have specific missions relative to drug enforcement in particular.

Since drug traffickers are particularly transient, adequate police jurisdiction is an important consideration in each drug investigation. Law enforcement must either possess the jurisdiction to pursue these criminals over a vast geographical area or be prepared to work with other agencies in the exchanging of information and resources. The different roles of drug enforcement will be discussed next.

INTERPOL

Due to the extensive global involvement of many smuggling operations, law enforcement agencies throughout the world can better communicate with each other through an organization known as the International Criminal Police Organization, or INTERPOL. This organization was etablished in 1923 and serves as a communication network between member countries wishing to identify international criminals. The agency itself does not employ sworn personnel with international police powers but acts as a network to exchange information between countries.

Each member country must establish a National Central Bureau that will act as that country's contact point for other members. In the United States, the National Central Bureau uses personnel from both the justice department and the treasury department.

The offenses investigated by INTERPOL and its members are many, including narcotics traffic, money laundering, financial fraud, and terrorism.

THE FEDERAL ROLE

The federal role in drug law enforcement is a crucial ingredient in the overall drug enforcement effort, due to the diversity and scope of drug law violations and the fact that many different agencies address varying aspects of the problem. Those federal agencies frequently involved in drug trafficking investigations are listed as follows:

a. Drug Enforcement Administration
b. Federal Bureau of Investigation
c. United States Customs Service
d. Internal Revenue Service
e. Bureau of Alcohol, Tobacco, and Firearms
f. United States Marshal's Service
g. United States Border Patrol
h. U.S. Coast Guard
i. U.S. Postal Inspectors

The above agencies represent only a few of the agencies which frequently become involved in the enforcement of drug law violations in the United States.

Certain federal agencies have basic responsibility for evaluating foreign involvement in the growing, manufacturing, and trafficking of illicit substances. The DEA, for instance, assigns agents all over the world to work with foreign drug enforcement authorities in collecting criminal intelligence.

The next responsibility of the federal arm of drug enforcement is to investigate "interdiction" activities, or the smuggling of drugs across American borders. Not all federal enforcement agencies, however, perform this function. One of the primary agencies enforcing interdiction activities is the U.S. Customs Service, which is an extremely active anti-smuggling component to the drug enforcement effort. For the most part, agencies who investigate "interdiction" activities, such as the U.S. Customs Service, are required to turn the case over to the DEA for investigation once the drugs enter the country and a seizure is made.

Domestic federal drug enforcement agencies operate under two separate branches of government: the Justice Department and the Treasury Department. Once drugs have arrived in the country, both the Drug Enforcement Admnistration and the Federal Bureau of Investigation have jurisdiction to conduct full criminal investigations into the origin of the substances, their trafficking patterns, and suspects involved in the operation.

The primary federal agency designated for drug enforcement, however, is the DEA. The FBI was granted drug enforcement authority in January 1982 to assist in overall drug enforcement strategies.

THE STATE ROLE

The state government role in drug enforcement is primarily to assist any jurisdiction within the state that has a local drug problem but cannot support a drug investigation unit of its own.

The involvement of state drug enforcement units serves as a highly significant factor in drug supression, and due to the broad jurisdiction and resources of most state agencies, thousands of drug traffickers are located, identified, and arrested every year. National drug arrest and conviction statistics would not be anywhere near what they are without the state drug enforcement complement.

Some state enforcement units may work as a specialized part of the state bureau of investigation, while other state agencies are created to address drug enforcement priorities exclusively. Typically, these state drug units are afforded many resources such as money, equipment, and training not easily acquired by local departments operating on a limited budget.

A few states still have no state criminal investigation bureau. In this instance, state highway patrol officers may attempt to fill the void, providing they have the statutory authority to investigate criminal law violations.

THE LOCAL ROLE (City/County)

In the overall drug-suppression effort, city police and county sheriff departments have the most important role of all. Although some agencies lack sufficient resources, most local law enforcement agencies have better criminal intelligence capabilities, which aids them in the performance of their duties. With the constant contact between law enforcement officers and local street criminals, local drug investigators are provided a steady stream of potential informers and up-to-date information regarding those who are criminally active in local drug distribution networks.

Typically, the main resource not as available on the local level is operational money for drug purchases, equipment, and additional manpower. This can amount to tens of thousands of dollars yearly.

In spite of varying police agencies from jurisdiction to jurisdiction, those who take on the task of drug enforcement face many of the same problems regarding manpower, training, and operational money. Agents also share similar personal afflictions in their chosen profession, including tension and job-related stress, which can sometimes result in considerable personal sacrifices.

THE PROSECUTOR

The county or district prosecutor's office is a vital component of any drug enforcement effort. Though not usually thought of as a law enforcement officer, the prosecutor or his assistants are responsible for the successful completion of the criminal drug case once the suspects have been arrested. The success of securing a conviction in a drug case, however, largely depends on how thoroughly prepared the case is when it is presented to the prosecutor for filing.

Law enforcement officers frequently complain about prosecutors who plea bargain drug cases prior to trial. This is when the defendant agrees to plead guilty to a lesser offense than charged in order to avoid the risk of receiving an extensive sentence from a jury or judge. This may occur when a prosecutor is unfamiliar with the elements of a particular crime or when an inexperienced prosecutor wishes to avoid time-consuming trial work. The plea-bargaining of a case may also occur when the case has been mishandled during the investigation process or is just not presentable, for any number of reasons, in a court of law.

The prosecutor, however, should be considered one of law enforcement's greatest allies, even during some criminal investigations. Those prosecutors who take a personal interest in each drug-related case can keep agents abreast of the legal and technical requirements of each investigation, resulting in a successful conviction of the drug offender.

CHAPTER 10

FUNDAMENTALS OF DRUG INVESTIGATION

THE INVESTIGATION of drug violations, like any other type of criminal act, may be pursued in a number of ways. The purpose of this chapter is to acquaint the reader with various investigative techniques, some of which might be considered standard operating procedure, while other techniques are more unconventional.

A successful drug investigation technique is one which affords the undercover officer and his fellow officers the optimal safety. Furthermore, it is a method of successfully accumulating evidence against suspected violators for criminal prosecution.

Each investigative phase discussed in the upcoming chapter should not be considered at face value, realizing that what works in one situation may not work in a similar situation. The elements surrounding each investigative inquiry often dictate individually specialized methods to be used.

As in any criminal investigation, regardless of methods used, consideration should always be given to officer safety throughout every phase of the investigation. Additionally, participating officers must be cognizant of their agency's policy, procedure, and the specific state and federal laws which govern their actions.

WORKING UNDERCOVER

When most people think of narcotics investigations, undercover work is frequently associated. The term "agent," however, is a general term used synonymously with detective or criminal investigator. While the deployment of an undercover agent is an effective investigative technique, it is only one method of many in which to investigate suspected drug violations.

Undercover work is considered a "pro-active" type of investigation as opposed to the traditional "re-active" role of most detectives. Again, this means that the undercover officer must "seek out" or locate suspected drug dealers who are actively engaged in the commission of felony acts, rather than locate and arrest one who has "already" committed a crime.

Used extensively by law enforcement agencies, undercover work provides the investigator the rare opportunity not only to observe a felony in progress but to actually be present when it is instigated and to collect evidence directly from the criminal himself.

Agents must take extreme care in this type of investigation to insure their own safety and to avoid legal pitfalls. For purposes of prosecution, however, state and federal law require police, in their investigation, to show the suspect's "criminal intent" in a violation. This demonstrates to the court that the suspect was "predetermined" to commit the act with or without the participation of the narcotics agent.

The end result is direct testimony from a certified law enforcement officer who can provide the prosecutor, jury, and judge fully documented, firsthand information about a crime. These cases are generally considered difficult to defend and will frequently lead to the successful conviction of a drug trafficker and hopefully provide a deterrent for others involved in criminal acts.

PERSONNEL

The selection of a candidate for an undercover assignment is a management decision involving many variables. First, a candidate's age, color, build, or sex may not play a big role in his or her overall performance on the street unless, of course, there is a particular need for one of those traits in the investigation. A person's initial motivation, however, must be examined and scrutinized to determine his suitability for this task.

An officer who has proven capabilities in working with minimum direct supervision or who has demonstrated a propensity to deal successfully with people from different walks of society might also prove to be a good choice.

The hours to be worked depend on the internal structure of the drug enforcement unit and should be made clear to the candidate for the job.

Many units work "shift work" with specific hours assigned, while other units work both day and night hours, or so-called "flex time," depending on the investigations at hand. In either scenario, the likelihood for overtime is almost inevitable, and dealing with this problem is done on an individual basis by each agency.

COVER STORY

Once the decision has been made to initiate an undercover investigation, the undercover agent must prepare himself for the street by considering a number of precautions.

First, a cover story must be established by the officer and/or his supervisor. The cover story is the agent's background story while he is on the street. This is the information he gives drug dealers about himself (name, address, home town, occupation, etc.) to help build credibility and a personal rapport with the suspected violator. It would be advisable for the supervisor to permit the agent to create his own story, so the agent can include variables with which he is personally familiar.

An assumed name must then be chosen by the undercover candidate. This will help insulate his personal life from the criminal underground and give confidence to the agent when working. Although not absolutely necessary, it is recommended that the agent select an undercover name that uses his actual first name but a fictitious last name. This is normally much easier to deal with than having to memorize a completely new name.

Occupations and home towns should always be those with which the agent is familiar. In other words, officers should not tell the dealer that they are a plumber if they do not know anything about the business of plumbing. As luck would have it, the suspect might be a former plumber himself. Additionally, officers should not say that they are from Chicago if the officer has never set foot in that town in his life. The suspect may make regular trips there or have friends there he can check with to verify the officer's story.

The drug enforcement unit itself should provide the agent additional props to help support his cover story, such as a fictitious checking account, social security card, and driver's license, only to name a few. These items strengthen the agent's cover story and help convince the suspect that the agent's story is genuine.

Once the story is decided on, investigational objectives must be established. This may be based on the availability of any confidential sources (informers) and their ability to introduce agents to known drug dealers or on general criminal intelligence of taverns or other places where drug activity is believed to take place.

Just where the agent works will dictate his clothing, mannerisms, language, and any other variables which pertain to his undercover identity. The agent must have the ability to transcend the role of a low-level street dealer to that of an upper-class drug financier, depending on the tasks at hand. This is to avoid any trait "carry-over" that might be considered out of character by the violator and cast suspicion on the agent.

It is always important for the agent to be aware of the current names for drugs and associated terminology. This street "lingo" is always in a state of change, and undercover agents must keep abreast of up-to-date terms to avoid seeming new to the street or naive. Remember, even if the dealer just thinks an agent is a police officer, without actually knowing for sure, the agent and the investigation are in serious jeopardy. The following is a very general list of street terms commonly used by drug dealers and users. Some violators use street language more than others, while the more sophisticated perpetrator might use more standard terminology.

STREET LANGUAGE

Acid—LSD
Angel dust—PCP in powder form (phencyclidine)
Bad trip—Bad experience when taking drugs
Bag—Usually refers to a one ounce quantity of drugs (usually marijuana)
Balloon—A small balloon rolled up and containing less than a gram of drugs (usually heroin)
Bennies—Amphetamines
Bindle—A small piece of folded paper containing approximately one gram of powder
Black tar—A form of heroin
Blow—Cocaine
Bong—A special pipe for smoking marijuana or hash
Bowl—A pipe for smoking marijuana or hash
Brick—A term referring to a quantity of compressed marijuana (usually 1 kilogram)
Brown sugar—Heroin

Buds—The flower tops of a female marijuana plant
Bummer—Unpleasant experience
Burnt out—Tired of drug use, or physically or mentally impaired from long-term drug use
Bust—An arrest
Buttons—The buds from a peyote cactus
Clean—To be free of drugs
Coke—Cocaine
Cold turkey—To quite drugs all at once
Connect—To locate a dealer to purchase drugs
Connection—A drug dealer
Cooker—One who operates an illegal drug lab
Cop—To purchase drugs
Crack—A type of inexpensive but potent freebase cocaine
Crank—Methamphetamine powder
Crash—Pass out or sleep
Crystal—Methamphetamine powder
Cut—To dilute
Dime bag—A quantity of drugs costing ten dollars
Dirty—To be in possession of drugs
Dope—Drugs
Downers—Barbiturates
Elbow—One pound (Lb.)
Dust—PCP powder
Fire—To inject drugs
Flake—Cocaine
Ganja—Jamaican marijuana
Get off—Under the influence of drugs
Gram—A one gram quantity of drugs (usually a powder)
Grass—Marijuana
Habit—Addiction
Hard stuff—Narcotics, e.g. heroin, morphine
Hit—To take a dose of drugs
Holding—In possession of drugs
Hooked—Addicted
Horse—Heroin
Joint—Marijuana cigarette
Junk—Heroin
Kilo—2.2 lbs.

L.B.—One pound
Lid—One ounce of marijuana
LSD—Lysergic acid diethylamide
Magic mushroom—Psilocybe mushroom (hallucinogen)
Mainline—To inject drugs
Micro dots—Small tablets of LSD
Narc—A narcotics agent or police informer
Nickel bag—A five-dollar quantity of drugs
O.D.—Overdose of drugs
O.Z.—One ounce quantity
Pot—Marijuana
Pusher—Drug dealer
Quarter—1/4 pound, or 1/4 ounce quantity
Quarter paper—1/4 gram of powder
Roach—Burnt marijuana cigarette
Rush—A sudden euphoric feeling
Script—A drug prescription
Score—To purchase drugs
Sinse—Sinsemilla (seedless marijuana)
Skag—Heroin
Skin popping—Injecting drugs immediately under the skin
Smoke—Marijuana
Smack—Heroin
Snort—To sniff powder
Snow—Cocaine
Spaced out—Under the influence
Speedball—Heroin and cocaine combination
Spoon—A small quantity of drugs (powder)
Stash—A hiding place for drugs
Stoned—Under the influence of marijuana
Strung out—Under the influence or addiction to a certain drug or combination thereof
Tea—PCP powder
Toot—Cocaine
Tops—The flowers of the female marijuana plant
Tracks—Scars from injecting drugs regularly
Trip—An experience with LSD
Uppers—Amphetamines
Wasted—Heavy drug intoxication

WEAPONS

Careful consideration must be given to the type of weapon carried by the agent who works undercover. Considerations such as concealment, accessibility, stopping power, and comfort are items which may make the ultimate difference in saving an undercover officer's life.

Agency policy plays a large role in this issue and might mandate a particular weapon. It is possible, however, that the agent might be permitted to carry a personal or special departmental weapon with which he can qualify for official use.

Many officers find that carrying a revolver is easiest due to earlier basic police training. Others prefer the flat and easily concealed semiautomatic handgun which will hold more rounds of ammunition and might possibly reload faster in emergency situations.

There is no longer any particular stigma attached to the carrying of a revolver or a semiautomatic with regard to the criminal's perception of the agent. If a dealer perceives the agent to be a "narc" (police officer) because of the type of handgun he carries, the agent must rely on his original cover story to convince the suspect otherwise, or advise the suspect that the gun was purchased as a stolen weapon for a cheap price and that the agent is not aware of its origin. It is common in the drug business to find criminals with either revolvers or automatic handguns, so the officer should concern himself with what weapon he will be most comfortable with on the street.

VEHICLES

Once again, an agency's policy and budgetary restraints will most likely determine what vehicles will be placed in service as undercover vehicles. If choices can be made, vehicles that are common in style and color (grey, white, tan, dark blue), and generally plain looking, will blend in much more successfully than flashy vehicles with loud paint jobs or other distinguishable features.

A flashy car might serve a purpose in a short-term undercover situation but will rapidly become useless during a moving surveillance. It could even jeopardize or "burn" the entire investigation if it were recognized or even suspected as a police vehicle. Officers should take care to be sure that any obvious physical damage to agent vehicles is repaired before conducting surveillance operations. This damage, as well as burned-out headlights, taillights, or even parking lights will give the suspects something to remember if seen more than once.

The installation of headlamp or taillamp "kill switches" in surveillance vehicles will usually aid support officers in nighttime stakeouts and moving surveillances. The switches may be used to temporarily extinguish single headlamps or taillights while agents are following suspect vehicles, giving the impression of different vehicles behind the suspect at different times.

Radios and all other official-appearing gear must be concealed to avoid the appearance of anything that can be associated with police work. The only items within sight inside the undercover vehicle should be items that the agent should expect the suspect to examine such as a checkbook or personal mail. Sometimes, it is advantageous to deliberately leave items associated with the agent's supposed line of work in view.

When going undercover, the agent must remember to shut off all police radios, scanners, and so forth, in the undercover vehicle. Failure to do so will result in alarming the perpetrator and placing the agent and the investigation in immediate danger.

It is a good practice to avoid contact with anything or anyone who might cause people to suspect that the agent is a police officer. For instance, official police gasoline and service areas or "motor pools" often are staffed with the perpetrators themselves or their friends, who might spread vehicle, license tag, and agents' personal descriptions to associates.

Progressive law enforcement agencies should always provide the ability for the undercover agent to conceal his identity throughout the investigation.

COMMUNICATIONS

Proper and reliable communications are an absolute necessity when considering any type of undercover operation. It is not only essential for the success of the overall investigation but, more importantly, to the safety of the undercover agents themselves.

"Car-to-base" radio considerations are vital in undercover work as in all other facets of law enforcement. This is the capability to stay in contact with a dispatcher for emergency situations requiring backup. Furthermore, car-to-base communications benefit field officers by relaying messages, criminal records, or other information the agents might request while they are in the field. This is of particular importance when a surveillance involves more than one police agency. In this instance, each agency should have the ability to communicate not only with each other but also with their own central dispatcher in the event of an exchange of gunfire or other unforeseen emergency during the surveillance.

Generally speaking, it is a good practice to refrain from discussing proper names, addresses, phone numbers, or details of an investigation over the air, especially if the radio channel uses a repeater. Many professional criminals, as well as radio, television stations and police enthusiasts, monitor these frequencies, many of which are published regularly in magazines and radio periodicals.

A channel that enables officers to communicate freely from "car to car" is an absolute necessity when working surveillance or discussing other investigative matters during an investigation. Many of the "monitoring" concerns are not as big a problem when using car-to-car radio, because a radio repeater is "not" being utilized. Caution, however, should always be exercised, just in case criminal suspects learn the car-to-car channel frequency.

In the case of broad jurisdiction where car-to-car communications must be used regularly and, consequently, a repeater must be used, a "scrambler" should be implemented. This devise is an add-on apparatus that literally scrambles the signal, rendering the monitoring useless because the conversations are totally inaudible to anyone not utilizing the scrambler attachment. Consequently, conversations made over the air, even on a repeater channel, "can" be monitored but are garbled and indistinguishable.

Walkie-talkies having the same car-to-base and car-to-car capabilities should always be at hand in case vehicles are used with no built-in radios. These are also utilized with their own built-in scanners for monitoring transmitters worn by undercover agents.

CASE DOCUMENTATION

As in any aspect of criminal investigation, the ability of the investigator to document any pertinent information relative to the case is essential. For the sake of this text, the assumption that case reports will be prepared regularly is understood, but officers should always be prepared to document additional or supportive information in the field when necessary to help strengthen their case.

The agent must be able to specify, verify, and reproduce field documentation in court later. Typically, field note taking is an adequate means of recording observations made by the agent or his support team. Circumstances will arise, however, requiring the agent to make recordings of conversations between suspected dealers, users, or informants. The success or failure of a case may be the difference in the jury having to take the "word" of a witness (officer or informant) about a drug conversation, or the jury actually listening to the "recorded" voice of the violator making incriminating statements.

Concealed transmitters or "body mikes" are the most typical means of audio surveillance used by narcotics agents. These devices are usually placed on the agent's (or their informant's) person where they cannot be detected by the suspect. Strategic placement of these devices will insure adequate transmission and reception of the audio signal for recording purposes.

Usually powered by batteries, the transmitter will only function successfully for so long. Once the transmitter is turned on, the best reception is during the initial thirty to forty-five minutes, even though the batteries themselves may last up to three hours. This is one reason why undercover contacts should be as brief as possible.

It is the responsibility of surveillance officers to monitor and tape-record any and all undercover contacts made by undercover operatives. The rule to follow should be "RECORD WHEN YOU CAN." Obiding by this rule of thumb could most likely save an investigation later on and could also make the agent's courtroom testimony much easier.

Normally, once the undercover contact has been concluded, the surveillance officer should punch the tabs out of the tape to prevent any accidental erasure of the tape. Secondly, he should initial the tape for evidentiary purposes (remember, this tape is evidence) and turn it over to the case agent, who must also initial it and store it for safekeeping. It is further recommended that a transcription of each tape be made by either the case agent or the secretarial staff and attached to the case report. This will aid the prosecutor later on.

The price of transmitters is sometimes prohibitive for smaller departments' budgetary considerations. In this case, the use of a miniature tape recorder may be substituted. Agents can purchase these at any number of electronics stores, and they should have the capability to be activated by a remote-control switch. These recorders should not have a warning signal or "beep" at the end of the tape.

The obvious drawback with a concealed tape recorder is that the surveillance officers cannot monitor the conversation while it's taking place. Even though the tape is still excellent evidence, the safety factor for the undercover operative is greatly diminished. With regard to quality, however, the fidelity of the miniature tape recording may actually be a higher quality than a "body-mike" recording.

Tape recorders may also be used when recording interviews or interrogations. It is not necessary to advise the person being interviewed that you are recording his conversation, and it would only serve to inhibit the subject, anyway. Federal law permits the recording of conversations by one of the parties involved without consent of the other parties. This can be accomplished either in person or telephonically by using an induction coil (suction-cup type) which may be purchased at most electronics stores.

It is only when a conversation is recorded, and "neither" party involved in the conversation is aware of the recording, that the subject's "reasonable expectation of privacy" is violated. Wiretaps and eavesdropping operations, however, may be fully authorized for law enforcement officers, provided they have obtained a lawful court order to do so.

Other forms of documentation frequently used by narcotics officers are the use of photographs and video cameras during surveillance. A photograph or videotape, like a tape-recorded conversation, is evidence that can hardly be refuted by the criminal suspects and their attorneys. The use of special telephoto, fiber optic, infrared, and night-viewing lenses often enhance details otherwise lost during some investigations and give the jury something to hold or examine during case presentation. It should be common practice to employ these devices in both outdoor contacts with dealers as well as inside meetings in specially "wired" undercover apartments or rooms.

Defense attorneys, however, will always attempt to suppress the above evidence during a suppression hearing. During this hearing, the defense tries to show that the evidence was illegally obtained by the police, in hopes that the judge will rule the evidence "inadmissible." If properly obtained, the drug investigator should experience no problems in the admissibility of this type of evidence.

CASE INITIATION

As mentioned earlier, the duties of narcotics agents involve a "pro-active" approach to criminal investigation, opposed to the traditional "re-active" method, meaning that agents initiate their own investigations rather than waiting for crimes to occur and then investigate them.

The initial phase of case initiation should include the reviewing of criminal intelligence files to identify problem areas of heavy drug traffic. These files contain an array of information such as names, nicknames, addresses, and occupations of suspected drug traffickers.

Realizing, of course, that much of the information contained in intelligence files is unverified, still much of it is valid and workable. Intelligence files are also useful in identifying names and addresses of suspected dealers. Agents may elect to conduct covert surveillance on these suspects or their residences to identify associates, vehicles, and general activity of the suspect. The amount of vehicle traffic to and from the residence, as well as criminal checks of visitors with criminal records, can help build probable cause that drug dealing is, in fact, taking place. Sufficient information in this area may be grounds for a search warrant to be served at a later time.

A close liaison with other law enforcement agencies can also be one of the criminal investigator's greatest allies in case initiation. It is through such working relationships that the exchange of information, investigative leads, and criminal informants becomes almost commonplace.

The following sources may provide valuable information on suspects during the course of an investigation:

The telephone company
Insurance companies
Utilities companies
Banks
Credit agencies
Labor unions
Transportation companies

The use of an undercover agent is an effective way of initiating drug cases. Although risky and time consuming, this technique can have its advantages. Identifying a tavern where suspected drug dealing is taking place will enable an agent to work inside the tavern undercover as a customer, verifying firsthand the suspicions of drug dealing. The agent may then choose to attempt drug purchases on his own or cultivate an informer inside the tavern to assist him.

The deployment of undercover agents working "solo" for the purpose of case initiation can be successful, but it does have three serious shortcomings.

1. The safety factor for the agent is greatly reduced due to the fact that other officers cannot easily cover the undercover agent's lengthy criminal contacts (Fig. 9).

Figure 9. The "buy-bust" is considered the most dangerous task in drug enforcement. The above photo is a blood-stained parking lot with an emptied police service revolver and the officer's "war on drugs" cap. The officer in this case was attempting to arrest a drug dealer and luckily survived a blast from a sawed-off shotgun. (Photo courtesy of the Oklahoma Bureau of Narcotics and Dangerous Drugs Control.)

2. The quality of cases developed will be almost strictly "street level" dealers who are not considered significant players in the total drug-trafficking picture. The only real benefit to initiating a case in this fashion is to purchase drugs from dealers and attempt to make informers or "turn them around" to work for the agent.
3. To associate regularly with suspected drug offenders requires a great deal of time and money.

Ultimately, the best method of initiating a drug case is to use a reliable informer who is known to drug-trafficking suspects. This will minimize the danger factor for the agent and expedite the overall investigation (see Chapter 7, "The Informer—A Profile).

THE BUY

A drug transaction between a narcotics suspect and an agent (or police informer) is probably the most traditional type of felony drug case made in the area of drug enforcement. This is certainly not the only way to collect evidence on drug traffickers, nor is it the most effective method of arresting higher-level dealers in the drug trade. What this practice does provide, however, is a chance for law enforcement officers to identify known traffickers and use each arrestee as a potential informant to locate drug violators higher up the ladder. This can be done with relatively little expense to the investigating police agency.

The drug buy, if administered properly, may be the strongest type of drug case there is with regards to prosecution. Prosecutors have little problem in trying a buy case in which there is a "hand-to-hand" delivery of a controlled substance from a suspect to a police officer. This is because fewer witnesses are needed to locate and testify once the case goes to court. This, consequently, makes coordination, organization, and presentation of the drug case much easier for the prosecutors than one involving a string of police or civilian witnesses.

THE BUY-WALK

This is the purchasing of drugs from a dealer by an undercover agent when there is no immediate plan to arrest the suspect. Investigations of this type can be quite expensive for departments with financial restrictions, but it can usually afford the undercover agent a chance to work up the ladder toward a more significant dealer and to identify others involved in the distribution network.

Extreme care should be taken by undercover agents as to the location of the buy in a buy-walk situation. The safety of the undercover agent and the surveilling officer's ability to adequately observe and record the transaction need to be considered.

Agreeing to meet drug dealers at locations of "their" choosing or on their "turf" strips the agent of his control of the situation and permits the dealers to arrange for countersurveillance or a location where a "rip-off" may occur. In negotiations for the buy, the agent must decide on which of the following "types" of buys should be pursued:

1. House buy
2. Car buy
3. Public place

The House Buy

The house buy could take place at a house or apartment where the police have specially installed covert audiovisual surveillance and recording systems. This is beneficial for both the recording and documentation of the transaction under optimum conditions, as well as providing the officer additional safety in case a problem arises during the buy. House buys can also take place at the residence of the dealer. When this happens, officers must realize that the dealer might have associates present at the residence, consequently diminishing the officer's level of safety. The benefit of a buy at the suspect's residence is that the agent will acquire much valuable intelligence about the suspect's residence, associates, and methods of concealment. Also, it might provide the probable cause needed to later acquire a search warrant.

The Car Buy

This is when the dealer meets the agent at a predetermined location, such as a parking lot. Strict agent discipline and total control of the situation must be practiced in this scenario. Under this circumstance, the agent should never agree to "go for a ride" with the dealer. Often, the dealer will suggest a trip around the block so the agent can examine the drugs and make the purchase while the suspect's vehicle is in motion. Once the agent agrees to do this, his safety is in serious jeopardy, because neither he nor the surveillance officers will have any indication where the suspect's destination is.

If the cars are stationary, the agent can request that the suspect sit in the undercover vehicle, thereby maintaining control of the situation. It is important in a car buy to completely document the suspect's use of his vehicle. This will aid in the forfeiture of the vehicle at the culmination of the investigation.

Public Places

In almost all circumstances, the agent should be the one who chooses the location of the buy. The strategic selection of the location will benefit both the agent and his surveillance officers at the time of the buy. The agent should always insist on a busy public place where fellow officers can mix unobtrusively and adequately "cover" the agent during the transaction.

When undercover agents meet dealers for a drug purchase, the key word to be remembered is "control." Even in a situation where the agent initially has control, many changes can take place where the dealers themselves assume control midway through the transaction without the knowledge of an unobservant undercover agent.

After the deal is underway, the agents should have mapped out a three-point plan specifying alternate locations for the deal if circumstances require a change of location during the deal. This plan will give the agent options that may ultimately save his life if the deal changes.

In cases when the dealer arrives at the agreed-upon location but wants to change to a different location, the agents should have the following prearranged contingency plan:

1. PLAN A. The agent should suggest a location (prearranged with fellow officers) where his surveillance can cover him and stay discreet, such as another busy shopping center parking lot.
2. PLAN B. When the suspect disagrees with the first suggestion and requests a second location, the agent should let the suspect make his suggestion and then counter it with an alternate suggestion of his own, another easily surveyed location prearranged by the agent and his surveillance.
3. PLAN C. CALL IT OFF! Regardless of the progress of the transaction, when the location for a drug deal is changed for the third time (for any reason), the agent should call the deal "off." Continuing the deal at this point may only confuse surveillance officers and lessen the agent's degree of safety. It can always be rearranged at a later time.

THE BUY-BUST

The buy-bust is a drug purchase between an agent and a suspect which the suspect is to be arrested at the time of the transaction. This method is common at the conclusion of the undercover investigation and is considered to be the most dangerous duty of a narcotics agent.

This situation is similar, in many ways, to that of a buy-walk but with a few important differences. First, an arrest plan must be decided on between the undercover agent and all other officers participating in the arrest. This plan will require all participating officers to be assigned specific duties to effectively complete the arrest.

The undercover agent, in this incident, must convey a specific signal to backup officers, which he will use at the time of the arrest. This signal can either be a physical sign, such as the taking off of a hat, or a verbal signal which could be a special word used during the undercover conversation to alert backup officers that the arrest is about to take place.

When the agent decides to effect his arrest, he must be sure that backup officers are on the scene in case of a violent confrontation by the suspect (Fig. 10).

Figure 10. The bullet-ridden and blood-spattered vehicle of a drug dealer in Woodward, Oklahoma. During this gun battle, state narcotics agent William Stewart was shot and killed while attempting to arrest a suspect during a 1-ounce methamphetamine drug deal. The suspect was not injured during the gunfight but was later convicted of first-degree murder and sentenced to life imprisonment. (Photo courtesy of the Oklahoma Bureau of Narcotics and Dangerous Drugs Control.)

WORKING INFORMANTS

Criminal informants are yet another valuable asset to assist the criminal investigator in his daily work endeavors. An informant can expedite the entire operation by offering undercover introductions between agents and suspected dealers, as well as providing up-to-date criminal intelligence and, therefore, probable cause for search warrants.

The largest hurdles in handling informants are typically the officer's attitude toward the informant, the method in which they are treated during the investigation, and the informant's incentive to provide accurate, reliable information.

In police work, informants are often referred to as "sources" or "CI's," which stands for "confidential informant" or "cooperating individual." It is common for inexperienced officers to refer to their informants as "snitches" or some other derogatory term while in the informants' presence, but this only demeans them and drastically reduces their willingness to cooperate.

As discussed earlier, informants have many profiles or motives. Each motive must be identified at the onset of each investigation so the agent will continually know how to deal with his informant. Probably, the most common motivation for an informant is the "fear" of going to jail after being arrested. When this is the case, police officers might term this individual a "hammered informant."

Let's look at an informant/agent relationship and examine some of the do's and dont's. After an interview is arranged with a potential informant, the following procedure should be followed in determining motives, general knowledge, and honesty:

I. Interview the informant for knowledge of drugs in general.
   A. Ascertain the informant's knowledge of the general availability of drugs; in particular, what type and quantity of drugs the suspects are dealing.
   B. Also, determine exactly what types of drugs the informant has used in the past and is currently using. Informants are frequently willing to render this information.

II. Take a separate statement from the informant regarding his personal knowledge of each suspect, as well as any personal observations he has made that might be considered important.

A. Details regarding the suspect's name, address, phone number, place of employment.
B. Vehicle description, associates/girl friends/spouse, places frequented by suspect.

III. Attempt to verify informant's information to establish his reliability.
A. Check utility registration for address, and registration for auto tag numbers.
B. Check informant's criminal record:
1. Check NCIC (National Crime Information Center).
2. Check law enforcement agencies wherever informant has previously lived.

It is extremely important, at this stage, for the officer to act in the following manner when dealing with informants:

1. Be fair.
2. Be truthful and make no promises or statements that cannot be kept.
3. Keep the informant in his place, but be tactful. Do not let him run the show.
4. Guide the informant in an undercover situation so that he does not entrap his suspect target.
5. Try not to let him know too much about you as the interviewer. The more he knows, the less effective you become.
6. The officer must not be tolerant of any crimes committed by the informant.
7. Be careful not to adopt the low moral standards of informants. Do not allow the informant to influence judgments made by the officer.
8. Beware of informants who are the opposite sex of the officer, because, if not managed carefully, they may compromise the officer or interfere with the investigation due to sexual advances toward the officer.

The following "ground rules" should be clearly understood by both the informant and the officer during the initial meeting:

1. **Method of payment (if any) for services rendered.** In the case of a mercenary informant, payment on a case-by-case basis is not a good idea. If this becomes knowledge during the trial, the defendant may

claim he was "entrapped" by the informant who was rigging drug deals just to make extra money for himself. Payments on a weekly or monthly basis are usually much more satisfactory.

2. **Procedures evolving from a subsequent arrest.** That is, determine if informant's testimony will be required or if relocation of the informant is necessary.
3. **General understandings regarding the following:**
   A. Inside buys
   B. Multiple buys
   C. Informant buys
   D. The cover story
   E. Method for introducing the agent to the dealer
   F. Negotiated quantities and prices of drugs
   G. Course of action against the informant in the event he commits any illegal activity or actions that may hamper the investigation

The agent's agency should adopt policy and procedure on the handling of non-typical informants such as:

1. Females
2. Minors under the age of 18
3. Persons on probation, parole, and conditional release
4. Unreliable informants

The following is a guide of how to handle a controlled informant purchase. These steps should be followed closely to insure that a completed case is prosecutable.

Controlled Buys

An informant buy or a "controlled buy" is one method of investigating drug violations when the undercover agent is unable to make the purchase or when the dealer will sell only to the informant. Although this method is not the most effective method of making cases, it is extremely beneficial in identifying drug traffickers, establishing probable cause for search warrants, and gathering extensive criminal intelligence on drug-trafficking patterns.

Some prosecuting attorneys are reluctant to file drug distribution cases resulting from controlled buys, because the informant might be required to later testify against the suspect. When this happens, defense attorneys will try to discredit the informant's testimony by bringing up any of the informant's former criminal convictions, increasing the likelihood for an acquittal.

The preceding problem associated with informant testimony might be avoided by making sure surveillance officers are able to identify the defendant at the time of the drug transaction. This can be accomplished by instructing the informant to set up the drug transaction in a public place, such as a convenience store or shopping center. In this circumstance, the officers should be able to later identify the dealer based on the officer's personal observations, as well as other documentation of the transaction such as photos and tape recordings of the dealer's conversations.

The following is a guide to handling controlled purchases and obtaining probable cause for search warrants. These steps should be followed closely to insure a case that is possible to prosecute and difficult to defend. It is recommended that the local prosecutor be aware of this procedure so prosecution strategies can be planned.

Technique for Informant Buys and Obtaining Probable Cause

I. Take detailed statement from informant regarding suspect information as names, addresses, vehicles, whether armed or not, what type of drugs dealer is dealing.

II. Ascertain as much information on the suspect as possible.
   - A. Check utilities.
   - B. Check criminal background.

III. Monitor all aspects of financial transactions.
   - A. Record serial numbers of any "buy money" to be used in the purchase before it is checked out to the informant.
   - B. Obtain a receipt for the money.
   - C. Initial and date the money list and store it for use later as evidence.

IV. Perform strip search of informant before each buy.
   - A. Make thorough search of all clothing, wallet, etc.
   - B. Also search body cavities, nose, ears, mouth, and rectum.
   - C. If informant is a female, have female officer perform general strip search, and have the cavity search done by a physician if available.

D. If electronic surveillance equipment is available, place transmitter on the informant so both the informant and the suspect can be monitored successfully. This will add credibility to the informant. Remember, after the CI has been searched, do not let him out of sight or he will have to be searched all over again.

E. Search informant's vehicle if he will be using it for transportation to the drug purchase.

V. Have the informant make a pretext telephone call to the suspect before the buy to establish that the deal is still on and to see if the dealer admits having the drugs on hand or is expecting a delivery from an associate. These conversations should be tape recorded by the officer and the tape should be kept as evidence.

VI. Attempt to set up buys in a familiar, populated area that can be successfully observed by surveillance agents.

A. Arrange buys so surveillance can be conducted in:

1. A shopping center parking lot.
2. A motel room selected by agents.

B. Avoid allowing the informant to control the selection of the location without the officer's knowledge or approval.

VII. Closely supervise the actual buy.

A. Have the informant go directly to the suspect while driving slowly and use turn signals to indicate direction of travel.

B. The informant should purchase the drugs as soon as possible and attempt to extract as much drug-related conversation from the dealer as possible, which should be recorded by surveillance officers.

C. Give the informant a maximum period of time to be inside the residence, i.e. thirty minutes, etc.

VIII. Supervise the informant after the drug transaction.

A. Maintain constant eye contact with the informant after he leaves the residence and follow him to a prearranged location.

B. Take the drugs and transmitter from the informant.

C. Strip search the informant and search his vehicle again to determine that he does not have any drugs or money on him.

D. Take a statement from the informant and have him include any conversations of interest between him and the dealer.

IX. On last buy, have search warrant ready for residence and be prepared to seize any vehicle that might have been used for drug dealing during the investigation.

CHAPTER 11

DOMESTIC DRUG SOURCES

IT IS estimated that over 75 percent of the illegal drugs consumed in the United States are smuggled in from foreign countries. We have already examined the international sources of cocaine, heroin, and marijuana, but there exist other drug sources that we cannot blame on our foreign neighbors. These sources are those of illegally diverted pharmaceutical and clandestinely manufactured drugs produced in the United States by underground chemists and marijuana cultivators.

Although the problem of clandestinely produced drugs such as LSD, PCP, STP, methamphetamine, amphetamine, mescaline, marijuana and other "bathtub" drugs has been a concern for quite some time, it has been addressed, up until recently, on a relatively small scale.

Due to spreading chemical technology within the drug trade, narcotics agents are acquiring extensive experience in the investigation of these illegal operations. Since the late 1970s more and more dealers actually produce, on a local basis, their own supply of drugs and, consequently, eliminate costly and risky importation and smuggling operations.

This chapter focuses on domestic manufacture and cultivation of illegal drugs and ways of countering these activities.

CLANDESTINE LABORATORIES

Since the late 1970's, a tremendous upsurge in methamphetamine, amphetamine, and PCP laboratory activity has been observed by drug enforcement authorities across the country. During raids on these labs, chemical precursors, laboratory hardware, and refined drugs have been seized by law enforcement officers. The lab problem seems to have affected the entire country, with concentrated activity in western, southern and southwestern states. For example, in Oklahoma only one clandestine laboratory was seized in 1981 compared to twenty-seven labs seized in 1984.

When examining the reasons behind this escalating criminal activity, it is helpful to understand the reasons why the drug trafficker is attracted to this type of criminal enterprise:

1. The logistical problems of international smuggling operations are not a concern in laboratory operations.
2. Fewer people need to be aware of or involved in the overall operation.
3. Laboratories may be moved or relocated on short notice.
4. Labs are usually located in rural areas less populated by law enforcement.
5. Profit margin is higher because fewer people participate in the operation.

As mentioned, these laboratories are usually found in isolated rural areas, mountain cabins, and trailer houses off the beaten path. This is due to the distinctive odor of the laboratory, which in some cases can be smelled for great distances. In recent history, however, many laboratories have been discovered within city limits and abandoned places of business within the inner city (Fig. 11).

The operations make use of a wide range of technology from the crude to the sophisticated, depending on the imagination and resources of the violator. Some arrestees are degreed biochemists who display considerable intelligence, while others are low-level street dealers experimenting with chemical formulas for short-term profits.

The timing and seizure of a clandestine laboratory must be done very carefully. If raided too soon, agents will net nothing, and if raided too late, the evidence may be gone.

The production process is often a lengthy one, and if investigators enter the lab too soon, the drug may not yet have reached its final stages of production. If this does occur, depending on how well agents have documented their investigation, charges of conspiracy to manufacture or possession of illegal chemical precursors could still be filed against the perpetrators. With the use of a reliable informant, however, the agents should be able to successfully raid the lab and seize the illegal product and related evidence without any problem.

Figure 11. An illicit methamphetamine laboratory raided in 1986 near Springfield, Missouri. The laboratory was believed to be one of the largest illegal labs in the country. (Photo courtesy of the Leclede County Sheriffs Department, Lebanon, Missouri.)

As indicated, many of the chemicals or precursors used to make the final product are, by themselves, illegal. The acquisition of these chemicals is probably the most difficult phase of setting up a clandestine laboratory operation. Often, the criminal will first manufacture his own precursors, since some of these chemicals are individually controlled, and then attempt to purchase those chemicals that are not controlled such as ether, acetone, and other solvents and reagents. Legitimate chemical distribution companies throughout the country are often targeted by lab operators as a source of the chemical precursors for the operation. Chemicals purchased are frequently done so under the name of a fictitious company that supposedly has a need for the chemicals (Fig. 12).

Figure 12. Hardware for a clandestine laboratory is difficult to acquire and extremely expensive. (Photo courtesy of the Leclede County Sheriffs Department, Lebanon, Missouri.

The drug manufacturers who purchase chemicals from such companies are often detected by either the employees of the companies or by law enforcement agents who might be scrutinizing chemical sales.

The violators also frequently travel from state to state and to different companies for chemicals and hardware alike. This is done to avoid having to purchase too many chemicals in one location, thereby alerting the company of criminal activity in an illegal laboratory. Even though many different chemicals are used for drug manufacturing, some primary chemical precursors required are as follows:

METHAMPHETAMINE HC1 – Ethyl Ether Solvent
Hydrochloric Acid
Hydrogen
Methlamine
Phenylacetone (phenyl-2-propanone)

AMPHETAMINE – Ethyl Ether
Formamide
Sulfuric Acid
Phenylacetone (phenyl-2-propanone)
Methanol

PCP (PHENCYCLIDINE) – Piperidinocyclohexane-Carbonitrile
Bromobenzene
Hydrogen Chloride-Anhydrous

The chemicals previously listed can give an idea of the complexity of laboratory activity and the knowledge required to successfully manufacture drugs. Some of the chemicals needed for synthesis are essential chemicals, while others are reagents, solvents, and raw materials essential for a successful "cook."

Raiding the Lab

Once a raid plan has been established for a laboratory, security precautions must be discussed to insure the safety of each officer. The raid can be extremely dangerous because many corrosive and volatile chemicals are used in the lab, creating the likelihood for explosion. In addition, the laboratory site may be rigged with booby traps designed to injure the police and alert the criminals.

It is recommended that a qualified chemist assist the agents in securing the laboratory after the initial assault. The chemist may further aid the agents in locating and seizing equipment and chemicals essential to prove the case in court. If raid officers are unable to locate a police chemist, they should observe the following precautions:

1. No smoking should be allowed on the lab site.
2. The laboratory operator (cook) should be present with the officers when securing the lab. He may be less likely to direct officers into a trap if he thinks there is the possibility that he could also be injured in an explosion.

3. Care should be taken when turning off electrical equipment. Stirring machines should be left alone until a chemist can be located.
4. Once the suspects are under control, nearby neighbors and bystanders should be evacuated from the lab site in case of an explosion.

Evidence

The collection and preservation of evidence is a crucial variable in the raiding of a clandestine laboratory. It is important that the proper evidence is seized for a successful prosecution and that dangerous chemicals are either properly preserved as evidence or destroyed. After chemical evidence is seized, standard practices of search and seizure should always be followed regarding:

1. The inventory of all items seized from the crime scene should be photographed before any dismantling of the laboratory takes place.
2. Any money located in or near the laboratory site should be confiscated for possible forfeiture.
3. Any records, such as utility bills, personal correspondence, or other documents showing ownership or residency of the lab site should be seized.
4. Evidence of booby traps should be documented and seized (photos and physical evidence).
5. Any weapons, records, recipes, address books, or other items considered significant to the criminal operation are seizable.
6. Any vehicles which were used in the operation of the laboratory, either to acquire hardware, chemicals, or to deliver drugs, should be seized and impounded.

It is common in larger laboratory operations for large 55-gallon drums of ether or other dangerous chemicals to be located. These should be seized as evidence and subsequent storage or destruction plans must be arranged.

Each law enforcement agency involved in this situation must use its own resources for this task. Occasionally, state universities or other institutions may have experience in the handling, storage, or disposing of dangerous chemicals and should be notified.

MARIJUANA CULTIVATION

The problem of domestically grown marijuana is increasing so readily in the 1980s that the United States is becoming a major producer of marijuana in its own right. Most of the marijuana produced domestically, however, is consumed by American drug users rather than smuggled out of the country. Growers of this illegal plant are constantly searching for new ways to improve growing techniques and enhance the potency of the product for greater profits. The three most common grades of marijuana produced domestically are called:

Commercial
Sinsemilla
Indian Hemp (Ditchweed)

The majority of the land used by growers is in rural settings where the marijuana can be concealed by thick forests and mountain slopes. Much of this land is owned by unsuspecting farmers whose large acreages prevent them from making frequent inspections of their property. Other areas favored by growers are densely wooded areas owned by the National Forest Service which cover broad areas and are seldom patrolled.

Marijuana farmers are tending to grow their crop on increasingly smaller plots of land to avoid detection from police spotter planes. Many times these plants are planted along rows of corn or other crops to blend in better with the terrain. It is also common for individuals to plant their marijuana along creek or river beds, providing the grower a constant source of water for irrigation purposes. Often when plots are discovered in such places, portable electric generators for electricity and small portable water pumps used to pump creek water to the growing site are also found.

More frequently, crops are being grown inside greenhouses, barns, or other structures. This makes detection more difficult and enables growers to harvest their crop on a more frequent basis each year.

Once the plant is harvested, however, it is usually processed on the growing site. This is when the leaves (shake) and flower tops (buds) of the plant are stripped of their stems and placed inside trash bags or "bricked" by a trash compactor or homemade hydraulic bricker. Marijuana produced in this fashion usually has a predetermined outlet for local distribution, and it is usually transported to its ultimate destination by vans, rental vehicles, and pickup trucks with camper shells.

The plots are usually planted between March and May and are often harvested by moonlight between August and October (or the first frost). An investigation of this type of criminal operation should never be taken lightly by investigators, since many growers will use sophisticated equipment such as walkie-talkies, police scanners, tripwires that trigger floodlights, sophisticated underground irrigation systems, and even employ the use of deadly booby traps designed to deter or kill trespassers.

It has been thought that the Mafia might try to control this type of activity, but law enforcement officers believe that it would be too difficult to accomplish. According to most authorities, no single organization is currently responsible for controlling domestic marijuana production in the United States. These criminals, however, are often organized into small, highly structured distribution networks that are successful drug-trafficking operations and formidable law enforcement targets.

One of the major problems associated with domestic marijuana production is that strict prison sentences are seldom given to growers, since this offense is not generally considered as serious as other types of drug trafficking. In reality, this source of criminal drug activity is every bit as significant in the overall drug picture as a smuggled planeload of marijuana or an underground chemical laboratory.

Let's now take a look at the three most common types of domestically grown marijuana.

COMMERCIAL GRADE. This type of marijuana is produced in areas where the male and the female marijuana plant are permitted to grow in the same location and the female plants have been fertilized. Most of the domestic marijuana consumed in the United States is the commercial strain. Frequently, the female plants in these plots will be marked with a small flag or even a red ribbon for easy spotting during harvesting. The THC content of this type of plant will usually average about 5 percent.

SINSEMILLA *(Cannabis indica).* This is considered to be the highest grade of marijuana grown domestically, and it is estimated that over 25 percent of the overall domestic marijuana crop is of this type.

The word "sinsemilla" itself means "without seeds" and is produced from "unfertilized" female plants in a controlled growing area where male plants are removed prior to pollination. When this is done, the female plants produce much more resin (THC) to attract male pollen and, consequently, produce a much more potent plant. The average THC content of this plant is about 7 percent.

INDIAN HEMP (Ditchweed). This type of marijuana grows the most abundantly throughout the United States and is considered to be the least potent of all. Ditchweed grows openly in fields, ditch banks, and along railroad tracks and is sometimes picked by small-time drug dealers for local distribution. The leaves of ditchweed, however, are sometimes used as a "cut" for more expensive marijuana. The physical characteristics of the plant are very similar to that of commercial, but the THC content is only about 0.14 percent.

The techniques for growing marijuana in sophisticated indoor greenhouses are somewhat varied but seem to focus on two popular methods of growing. They are cloning and hydroponics and are explained as follows:

CLONING. This is a process where growers cultivate marijuana and then select the most superior plants. Part of the selected plant is then removed and soaked in a root stimulant and nurtured until it grows its own roots. This process permits growers to use only a select few plants rather than waiting for a new crop to seed.

HYDROPONICS. This is another process where a greenhouse is used to create optimal growing conditions for the plant. Technically, it is the science of growing plants in a soil-free solution and is most commonly used for growing tomatoes and cucumbers.

To combat the spreading menace of marijuana cultivation, drug enforcement officials depend on such legal tools as search-and-seizure laws pertaining to plain view, as well as forfeiture laws to seize personal assets and reduce the overall profit margin for this type of criminal. Furthermore, the use of fixed-wing spotter planes and four-wheel-drive vehicles by drug enforcement agents has enhanced eradication efforts. In recent years, the National Guard has offered manpower and equipment for local and state law enforcement agencies in domestic marijuana-eradication projects. These enforcement maneuvers are exhausting and may take up to several days at a time to complete.

Training for drug agents, National Guardsmen, and reserve police officers for these eradication projects must include information on what to do in case of snakebites, hornet stings, and heat exhaustion, which are problems frequently encountered in this type of strenuous activity.

Investigators have now recognized the potential danger of a cultivated marijuana-growing operation and have identified several signs that might indicate illegal activity in this area. Itemized below are some activities that might help profile a marijuana-growing operation:

1. An unusual amount of vehicular traffic, usually at night, transporting numerous individuals to and from the site, through entrance gates that are always locked after entry.

2. Individuals with no knowledge about farming or ranching, and with no visible means of support, purchasing land which would be well suited to the growing of marijuana.
3. Construction of a large greenhouse or tin building in an abnormal setting, where that type of building would not normally be used.
4. A house out in the country where males are seen going in and out and where females and children are rarely seen.
5. The establishment of camper trailers, tents, or recreational vehicles in a wooded area where there are no recreational activities.
6. Individuals purchasing large quantities of fertilizer, chicken wire, PVC pipe, garden hose, varying sizes of pots, stepladders, and camouflage clothing.
7. Unexplained and unseasonably high utility bills.

BOOBY TRAPS

Criminal activity associated with drug traffic is also directly associated with an alarming degree of violence. This violence might result from criminals wishing to inflict harm on other drug criminals for any of a variety of reasons. It is becoming more evident, however, that these acts of violence are often directed toward the police in the form of booby traps in order to deter detection or aid the violator in an escape.

Law enforcement authorities strive to familiarize themselves with these devices in order to make detection of them easier during a raid situation. Typically, these traps are used by criminals at both marijuana plots and clandestine laboratory sites alike. Listed below are the purposes for the installation of a booby trap:

1. To stop an individual from entering an area by injuring or killing him.
2. To warn the property owner of intruders on the premises.
3. To permit the violator an opportunity to escape by slowing down or stopping the police.

Most of the booby traps found in the United States are of basically two types: impaling or explosive. These devices can be activated by any number of methods, some of which are manual and others which are activated by the victim (Fig. 13).

Law enforcement officers are always encouraged to stay off trails leading into suspected areas that may be booby trapped. Such trails are the most common area where traps have been located.

Figure 13. An explosive booby trap secured to a tree with electrical wires attached to both sides of a clothespin. In this case, when an intruder steps on the "tripwire" (see arrow), a piece of wood is pulled out of the clothespin and the electrical connections are made, detonating an explosive device. (Photo courtesy of the Arkansas State Police.)

It is common to find the use of tripwires that are practically invisible to the naked eye. These are used to trigger explosive devices intended either to merely alarm the trespasser or possibly to injure or kill him.

Listed below are a few booby traps that have been located at marijuana cultivation and clandestine laboratory sites in the United States:

IMPALING TRAPS

1. THE PUNJI-PIT, commonly used in Vietnam, is a pit containing sharpened wood or metal stakes that are usually soaked with a poison

such as antifreeze or even urine. This trap does more than just injure, it can kill!

2. THE TROTLINE is a nearly invisible monofilament fish line with fish hooks suspended at eye level. This trap probably will not kill a person but could inflict serious permanent bodily damage.
3. THE VENUS FLY TRAP, also a common trap, is composed of a large tin can containing straightened fish hooks, nails, or other spikes secured inside the can and aiming downward. The can is commonly anchored in cement in the ground where it does not show. When the trap is stepped on, the foot cannot be removed without first cutting the spikes off.

EXPLOSIVE TRAPS

1. THE MOUSE TRAP is a device which, as the name implies, uses a mousetrap as a detonator. The trapwire is bent to form a firing pin that, when activated by a tripwire, strikes a shotgun shell attached to the end of the trap. Sometimes, pipe sleeves are added for additional fragmentation and injury.
2. THE FOOTBREAKER is a bullet placed inside a pipe that is placed face up in the ground. When someone walks on the bullet, the downward pressure forces the bullet to press against a nail that acts as a firing pin, and the result is a bullet wound in the foot.
3. THE HOT PLATE is a remote-controlled device that is a standard hot plate sitting in a plastic bag containing ether-soaked rags. The trap can be activated when the plate is plugged in by using a long extension cord.

Narcotics agents are forewarned about the possibility of these types of devices and should be trained to deal with them. Sadly, innocent trespassers such as hunters have inadvertently wandered into such areas and have consequently sustained grave injuries.

Other hazards frequently encountered by drug agents are sentries and snipers, often armed with rifles, automatic machine guns, and even attack dogs who roam the wooded area in and around a marijuana patch or illegal laboratory. Investigators in Oklahoma and Kansas have even encountered rattlesnakes, with rattles removed, tied to marijuana plants on pathways of marijuana patches.

PHARMACEUTICAL DRUG DIVERSION

As mentioned earlier, the three primary reasons illicit drugs are available in the United States are smuggling, clandestine laboratories, and the diversion of legally made drugs. In this section we will examine the problem of diversion and learn how violators succeed at this type of criminal endeavor.

It is estimated that at least 20 percent of all illicit drugs consumed in the United States are legitimately manufactured drugs intended for use as medical treatment. This is to say that a certain type of drug violator is "diverting" drugs from legal channels onto the street for profit.

Even though many agencies regulate manufacturers and distributors, narcotics agents will occasionally have to investigate physicians suspected of diverting drugs.

Physicians who involve themselves with this criminal activity often use two main methods of diversion:

1. Selling directly to the customer, who is usually an addict or other type of opportunist.
2. Ordering large amounts of drugs on the basis of his medical registration (DEA registration number) and acting as a broker for non-registered dealers in the illicit market.

The investigation of this type of criminal act poses a unique challenge for the narcotics agent. The agent must first establish that there was no doctor/patient relationship between the doctor and the recipient of the drugs. Secondly, it must be established that a controlled substance was, in fact, criminally distributed. An alternate method of investigation is to look for a record-keeping violation as a result of an audit of the physician's drug inventory (Fig. 14).

Other methods of diversion involve violators who attempt to use unsuspecting physicians by "walking scripts." This is done by claiming to have an ailment which does not really exist or forging a physician's handwriting on a blank prescription and presenting it to a pharmacist. Legal handlers of drugs or registrants have the responsibility of looking for these scams, but many registrants are easily fooled (Fig. 15).

The types of drugs most commonly sought by violators are painkillers (narcotics) and various sedatives (depressants). The market for speed (amphetamines), however, is still a problem in many areas. The diversion investigation is a complicated one in which the investigator must create a "paper trail" and trace order forms and prescriptions

TIME: January 1, 1979 to March 31, 1980 (15) months

DRUG	PURCHASED	DISTRIBUTED	ON HAND	SHORTAGES	%
PRELUDIN, 75 mg.	2,700 tabs	210 tabs	9 tabs	-2,216 tabs	-82.07
DILAUDID, 4 mg.	3,900 "	218 "	151 "	-3,081 "	-79
VALIUM, 2 mg.	8,500 "	496 "	938 "	-8,004 "	-94.16
VALIUM, 5 mg.	65,700 "	32,968 "	85 "	-25,067 "	-38.15
VALIUM, 10 mg.	407,300 "	12,781 "	1,665 "	-386,584 "	-94.9
CITRA FORTE	5,949 pts	14.38 pts	4 3/16 pts.	-5,915 pts	-99.44
DEMEROL, 50 mg.	500 tabs	572 tabs	74 tabs	+336 tabs	+67.2
DEMEROL, 100 mg.	600 "	272 "	31 "	+83 "	+13.8
DEXADRINE, 5 mg.	1,100 "	1,100 "	200 "	+10	+.01
DILAUDID, 2 mg.	600 "	692 "	0	+92	+15.3

Figure 14. Results from a pharmacy audit in 1979 showing massive shortages of such dangerous drugs as Preludin, Dilaudid and Valium. Note where overages of Demerol, Dexedrine and Dilaudid (2 mg.) indicate pharmacist's attempts to adjust his books but over-compensated quantities of drugs. (Photo courtesy of the Oklahoma bureau of Narcotics and Dangerous Drugs Control.)

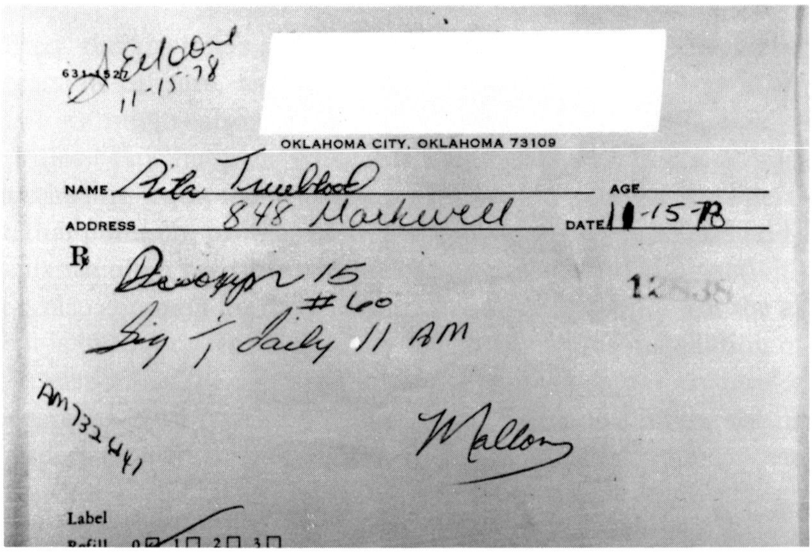

Figure 15. A forged prescription showing altered date, type of drug (Desoxyn) as well as different pens used for patient's name and address. (Photo courtesy of the Oklahoma Bureau of Narcotics and Dangerous Drugs Control.)

and have the ability to scrutinize records kept by all types of registrants (Fig. 15).

A definite correlation exists between the abuse of controlled substances by physicians and the likelihood of criminal diversion by this type of individual. In 1984, a study of 500 practicing physicians and 504 medical students was conducted by the Harvard School of Public Health and later published in the September 25, 1986, *New England Journal of Medicine.* The study found that more than one-third of physicians under the age of forty used drugs during their medical training and continued to use drugs (mostly marijuana and cocaine) afterwards. The study further articulated that an appreciable, although small, percentage of persons entering medicine have histories of extensive drug use and dependence. Older, established physicians often experience problems of alcoholism and drug abuse due to practices of self-treatment with tranquilizers and addictive painkillers such as opiates. For those investigators involved with cases of criminal diversion, the findings of the above study are not surprising.

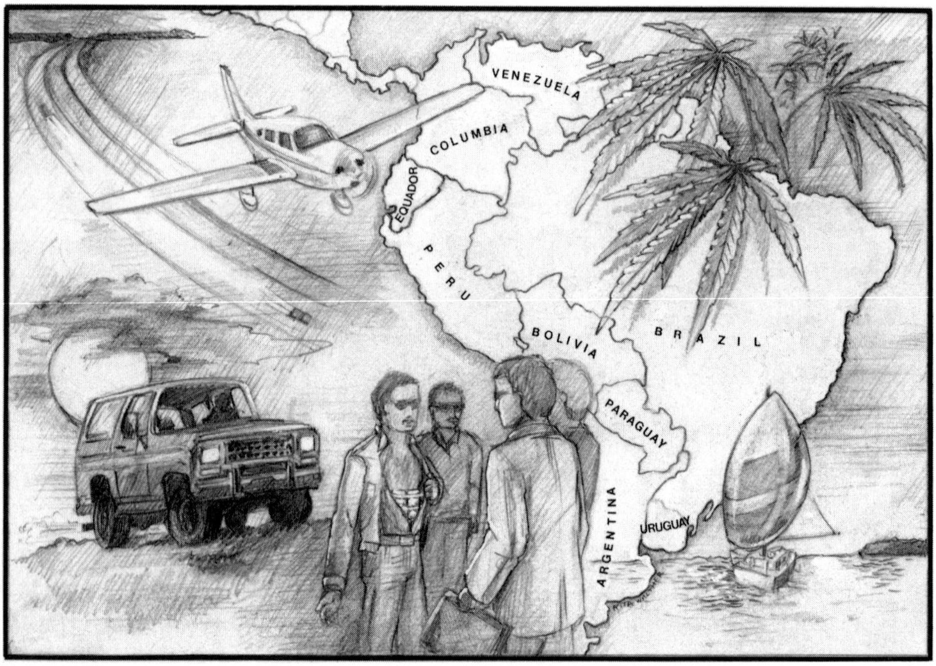
VENEZUELA
COLUMBIA
EQUADOR
PERU
BOLIVIA
BRAZIL
PARAGUAY
ARGENTINA
URUGUAY

CHAPTER 12

SMUGGLING ACTIVITIES

ONE OF the more perplexing tasks in drug enforcement today is the investigation of drug smuggling patterns used by modern-day traffickers. Those smugglers who undertake such a profession are often as skilled as their drug-producing counterparts, and the operations of both can be extremely difficult to detect.

Smuggling, simply defined, is the importation or exportation of any illegal commodity. There are as many ways to smuggle drugs as the imagination can fathom, and typically these methods fall somewhere within one of the following categories:

1. Aircraft—private/commercial
2. Marine
3. Ground vehicle—car/truck/trailer/etc.
4. Body packing

More drugs are now smuggled into the United States than ever before in history. According to federal statistics, the 150 tons of cocaine smuggled into the country in 1986 doubled that of 1985. Heroin importation reached an estimated twelve tons in 1986, up two tons from 1985, and an estimated sixty-five tons of marijuana were brought into the country in 1986, also up from 1985 by six tons. Drug enforcement authorities estimate that approximately 90 percent of the illegal drugs entering the country are going undetected.

Due to recent Federal Drug Task Force concentration on ports of entry such as the Gulf of Mexico coastline of Georgia, Alabama, and Louisiana, as well as the Atlantic coastline of Maine, Delaware, and North Carolina, traffickers have sought alternative routes and methods by which to smuggle their drugs into the country. Evidence of this can be found in a 1986 investigation that resulted in the arrest of twenty-three employees working for Eastern and Mexicana airlines. In this case the employees had smuggled as much as $1 billion of cocaine over a period of four years through Miami International Airport and had arranged as many as two loads a day during that period of time. The cocaine was believed to have come from the Colombian cities of Cali, Bogota, and Barranuilla.

Increased marijuana and heroin traffic has been noted along Mexico's 2,000-mile border, and the border patrol agents who combat this problem constantly complain about their lack of adequate equipment and manpower. Compounding the problem is that, as of 1977, it was concluded by the Drug Enforcement Administration that there are over 2,300 airstrips in Mexico, most of which are available to smugglers.

There are three basic venues of smuggling used by traffickers in the United States, which are listed as follows:

1. **International.** The transportation of contraband across international borders.
2. **Interstate.** The transportation of illicit substances for distribution between states.
3. **Intrastate.** The trafficking of drugs within the geographical area of a particular state.

Because these venues have their own unique characteristics, particular methods of smuggling are favored in each. We will now examine each of the methods of smuggling that are most frequently used by traffickers throughout the world (Table 9).

Table 9

Cocaine Seizures from Various Conveyances 1984
(% of total volume)

Land Transportation:	1%
Commercial Vessels:	8%
Non-Commercial Vessels:	11%
Commercial Air:	18%
General Aviation Aircraft:	62%

Source: President's Commission on Organized Crime, *America's Drug Habit,* Report to the President and the Attorney General, March 1986.

AIR SMUGGLING

Federal, state, and local drug enforcement officials are constantly fighting to stay abreast of air smuggling patterns and techniques. The majority of illegal drugs entering the United States are probably delivered by aircraft, since an airplane can travel much faster than a ground vehicle. The chances of aircraft drawing attention are slim, because most law enforcement officials do not know what signs to look for that might indicate smuggling activity.

The size of an aircraft may be indicative of a smuggling operation, although both large and small aircraft have been used extensively by smugglers over the years. Larger aircraft, for instance, are commonly used to import marijuana, while smaller planes are often used for bringing in quantities of cocaine. As in everything else in the drug business, these generalizations are not set in stone, and as soon as one pattern or trend is identified, a new one is established by the traffickers.

The smaller planes used may be as small as a Cessna 210, 206, or the popular Cessna 172 and 182 models. These planes are small, high-wing aircraft with about the same cargo area as a large van or pickup truck. This type of plane is relatively inexpensive but is much slower than a twin engine and may require refueling during its return trip.

Other popular aircraft commonly used by smugglers are twin-engine aircraft such as the Aerocommander and the Aztec which are significantly more expensive but much faster.

When using smaller aircraft, compared, for instance, to a DC 10, smugglers realize that they cannot haul large shipments of certain drugs such as marijuana, due to the bulk weight of the cargo. Smaller aircraft can, however, transport as much as 200–300 kilograms at a time (approximately 500–600 pounds).

Many aircraft seized by authorities are less expensive older planes. These are preferred by some traffickers because they can be abandoned in the case of a raid by law enforcement officers. Another technique is to lease aircraft for short-term trips. This practice lessens the chance that the aircraft can ultimately be seized by drug enforcement agents, cuts down on the traffickers' initial investment, and causes the aircraft to be less readily identified as a smuggling aircraft.

Air smugglers are often concerned about the capability of an aircraft to travel from the point of origin, such as Mexico, to its ultimate destination city within the United States. The risk of being detected is much greater with each fuel stop made by the pilot. Factors to be considered are the size of the aircraft and its fuel consumption ratio as well as the weight of the cargo being smuggled, which directly affects the plane's fuel consumption and endurance.

Since the border cities have recently been inundated with federal drug task forces, many smugglers have been forced to bring their payloads further inland. This creates problems with fuel consumption and usually requires the traffickers to install what is known as a "bladder tank." A bladder tank is a reserve fuel tank installed somewhere on or in the aircraft itself. These tanks are usually crude in nature but may be installed with some degree of proficiency. A bladder tank can be as makeshift as a waterbed located in the rear passenger compartment or as sophisticated as a metal fuel tank permanently installed in the aircraft by a professional aircraft mechanic.

The tank itself, when installed in an aircraft, is illegal unless a permit is acquired through the Federal Aviation Administration (FAA). Most smugglers avoid acquiring a permit, because they do not want to be on record as having a need for a bladder tank in the first place. Once the plane has been "plumbed," it is ready for the smuggling journey. Occasionally, police will locate aircraft still containing the entire drug payload, abandoned in isolated fields, because the plane ran out of fuel and was unable to meet the ground crew at the designated location.

When authorities are watching a plane, it is important to document the time of departure and direction of travel to help determine its return time. The pilot might decide to leave the United States at just about any time of the day and will probably plan on staying in the destination country a couple of days before returning.

Much can happen between the time the plane takes off and the time it returns with its illegal payload. For instance, the pilot may have trouble making connections, there could also be mechanical trouble with the aircraft, or the pilot may suspect that he is being watched by police and decide to terminate the trip.

In one instance, an aircraft being watched by narcotics agents in Oklahoma flew to Mexico for a load of marijuana. The night before he was to return to the United States, he got drunk in a Mexican pub. When the next day came, his hangover was so severe that he clipped one wing off of his plane during takeoff and crashed.

In some instances, the pilot lands his plane at a designated airstrip in Mexico or South America and is met by the traffickers at that location.

The traffickers then take the aircraft and fly it to an undisclosed location leaving the pilot behind. The drugs are then loaded in the aircraft and returned to the pilot later that day or the following day.

When aircraft do return to the U.S. with drugs, the strategic planning of a clandestine airstrip for landing and off-loading is another major concern. Landing at a major airport, or even a smaller air park, is physically safer but often riskier. Police or inquisitive fixed-base operators (FBO's) might then observe the people who meet the plane, known as the "ground crew." The ground crew work closely with the smugglers and usually drive vehicles such as trucks with camper shells, vans or other vehicles easily profiled by law enforcement officers and will be awaiting the arrival of the aircraft.

Many pilots prefer to use out-of-the-way roads, highways, or even fields that have been previously plotted by the traffickers. In these instances, the ground crew (usually two vehicles) might illuminate the designated landing strip with vehicle headlights or by using safety flares to guide the approaching aircraft. The use of ground-to-air radios is also common in smuggling operations. This enables the ground crew to communicate with the plane when they are close enough to do so.

It is frequently difficult for law enforcement officers to determine which channel the smugglers are using, since there are over one hundred available channels from which the traffickers may choose.

Once the pilot has landed and has met with the ground crew, the off-loading begins. This can take anywhere from five minutes to an hour, depending on the size of cargo. After off-loading, the pilot takes off and the ground crew heads, via the highway, to the local trafficker for packaging and distribution. It is from this point on that the domestic distribution process takes place (see Chapter 6, "The Drug Dealer—A Profile").

It is significant to note here that the pilot in a smuggling scheme might or might not know details about the overall smuggling operation. That is to say, the pilot could be hired to simply fly the plane for a prearranged fee. Sometimes, however, the pilot is the brains behind the distribution network and is familiar with players on every level of the smuggling operation. In this case, if caught, the pilot might be an excellent candidate for an informer to assist drug enforcement agents in their investigations.

The profiles mentioned earlier are with reference to certain physical characteristics of a smuggling aircraft. These characteristics arise as a result of adverse weather conditions, improper landing facilities and a general effort on the part of the violator to cloak his illegal activities. Some of the more common characteristics are as follows:

1. Chipped paint on propeller from landings on dirt roads.
2. Rear seats removed for additional storage space.
3. The installment of a bladder tank.
4. Covered windows.
5. Leaking break fluid around landing gear.
6. A pilot who pays for gas and repairs with cash.
7. Evidence of tampering with the "N" number.
8. Navigational charts and maps of source drug countries.

The investigation of smuggling operations frequently involves a considerable amount of surveillance on the part of drug enforcement agents. This may involve weeks or even months of twenty-four-hour-a-day observation.

Often, the airplane's physical characteristics will be observed by law enforcement officers, as previously mentioned, but the ground crew themselves might also be identified and subsequently watched by authorities. This happens when suspected individuals are documented as purchasing equipment commonly used in smuggling operations. From that point on, profiles of their vehicles are observed and additional surveillance often reveals associates and related smuggling activities.

It is also common for drug enforcement agents to monitor the aircraft while it is in flight. This is done by the surreptitious installation of a covert "transponder" in the aircraft, which emits a signal or "blip" on the radar screens of air traffic controllers. Once observed by the controllers, the suspect aircraft is immediately reported to the proper law enforcement authorities. This reported information includes coordinates, direction of travel, altitude, approximate speed, and other information considered pertinent. These devices are placed in the aircraft pursuant to a lawful court order and are considered to be a significant aid in smuggling detection.

GROUND SMUGGLING

Ground smuggling usually refers to the use of automobiles, trucks or other vehicles for the transporting of drugs or other contraband. The term, however, does not necessarily refer to importation of drugs "into" the country. Ground vehicles and aircraft for that matter are responsible for millions of dollars of interstate and intrastate trafficking once the drugs arrive in the United States. The investigation of ground smuggling activities, like air smuggling investigations, also requires considerable surveillance by drug enforcement agents. This type of observation will aid officers in the profiling of vehicles used, identifying suspects, and locating residences and other resources which might later be seized by drug enforcement agents.

Drugs are brought into the country through those states that commonly share the border with Mexico, such as California, Arizona, New Mexico, and Texas. Even though officials in these states are increasingly concerned about the problem of smuggling, the U.S. Border Patrol has the primary enforcement responsibility for the border areas.

Many of the drug-carrying vehicles that enter the United States enter through regular ports of entry and undergo routine inspections by U.S. Customs officials. For this reason, smugglers must exercise more caution to avoid detection. Ground vehicles do not have the same telltale signs as smuggling aircraft and are usually more difficult to profile.

By the use of false-bottom gas tanks, hidden compartments, and other inventive methods of concealment, many criminals can successfully bring their drugs into the U.S. without detection.

The United States Customs Service, however, has a tremendous enforcement tool at their disposal. Simply put, the Customs Service is one federal agency that may search a person or vehicle upon entering the country without a search warrant. The customs search enables officials to completely inspect a person or vehicle based on as little as a hunch.

Some of the typical areas used by smugglers to conceal drugs are listed below:

1. **Bumper, grill, and radiator areas.** Drugs can be attached by duct tape or magnetic container to rear of license plates or front bumper.
2. **Fenders and front wheels.** Drugs can be put inside or behind the hubcaps, or inside the headlight or parking-light assemblies.
3. **Motor area.** Drugs may be hidden in air filter, or attached to electric wiring or hoses; also, in windshield washer container or ventilation ducts.
4. **Cowling and dashboard areas.** Drugs can be hidden under floor mats, in hidden compartment in floorboard, or attached to outside surfaces of glove box.
5. **Header area.** Drugs can be put under fabric of header or sunvisor.

6. **Front seat area.** Drugs might be put between springs of front seat, under front seat, or within upholstery.
7. **Door paneling.** Drugs may be hidden in cut out portions of paneling.
8. **Back seat area.** Drugs can be placed under floor mat or in seat cushions.
9. **Rear fender and bumper area.**
10. **Trunk area.**

Figure 16. Marijuana was stored in these truck panels and ground-smuggled from El Paso, Texas to Enid, Oklahoma in 1985. (Photo courtesy of the Oklahoma Bureau of Narcotics and Dangerous Drugs.)

In 1984, New Mexico State Police and U.S. Customs agents documented the off-loading of a quantity of marijuana from a small aircraft to a large trailer. This trailer was then towed by one suspect driving a pickup truck. The truck and trailer were then followed to Oklahoma City, where the driver was arrested and 300 pounds of high-grade marijuana was confiscated from the trailer. The truck and trailer were subsequently seized by authorities and the suspects, along with four other co-defendants, were ultimately convicted of drug smuggling.

Figure 17. Although only 50 pounds of marijuana were smuggled at a time in this operation, dealers made trips twice a month to Enid, Oklahoma and were considered by authorities to be a significant drug source. (Photo courtesy of the Oklahoma Bureau of Narcotics and Dangerous Drugs.)

Figure 18. On a cold January night in 1985, narcotics agents from U.S. Customs, Texas, and Oklahoma seized this motor home which was ground-smuggling 285 pounds of high-grade marijuana in a hollowed-out gas tank. The marijuana was driven directly from Mexico to Oklahoma City. (Photo courtesy of the Oklahoma Bureau of Narcotics and Dangerous Drugs.)

MARINE SMUGGLING

If you have ever been to the Florida Keys, you have probably noticed the popularity of boating in that area. Actually, the sea is peppered with hundreds of small boats and ships. Not all of these boats, however, are for recreation.

The detection of smuggling vessels is also somewhat difficult, as suspect vessels might not fit a particular profile. When drugs are brought to the U.S. via sea, the initial vessel, known as the "mother ship," will usually stay out in international waters, free from U.S. search authority. Smaller boats will then meet with the mother ship to collect the drug cargo and bring it back into the United States shores. It is common that many smaller boats will meet the mother ship during a certain period of time. This allows each boat to carry a smaller payload that is easier to conceal. The large numbers of small boats in and around areas such as the Florida Keys make it difficult for drug enforcement agents to locate suspected vessels. When located, marine smugglers have been found to use the following areas of concealment:

1. In hollow masts and guardrails.
2. In areas between the deck and the hull of fiberglass boats.
3. Around fuel and water tanks.
4. In any reclosable containers such as paint cans.
5. In fuel tanks (if tank isn't full, it should alert officers when the crew claims to have been at sea for a long time).
6. Behind removable paneling.
7. In scuba tanks submerged below the waterline.

When raiding a vessel, agents should always attempt to get below as soon as possible to locate washbasins and sinks and identify residue of slushed out contraband.

In addition to marine smuggling activities, it is important to note that much smuggling is also done along rivers and lakes within the country and is considered to account for a significant amount of interstate smuggling activity.

BODY PACKING

The term "body packed" means the transportation of drugs by carrying them on one's person. This can be accomplished by simply placing the drugs in clothing pockets or taping packets of drugs directly on arms or legs. Another method is the actual swallowing of drugs that have been placed in some type of non-digestible container such as a balloon or condom.

For the most part, the drugs that are usually body packed are powders such as cocaine and heroin, but other drugs may be smuggled as well. This is because powders are more easily concealed, for example, than small amounts of marijuana or hashish. Body packing is commonly attempted when drugs are being moved through commercial channels such as airlines, bus lines, and trains. This method is somewhat successful as far as detection is concerned but is only good for the introduction of small amounts of drugs.

When the smuggled powder is placed in a balloon, it is frequently swallowed by the perpetrator and retrieved later either by vomiting or sifting through the smuggler's solid waste. This method is common in the introduction of drugs into jails and penal institutions.

The methods for body packing are not necessarily all that sophisticated. For example, a common method for transporting a one-pound quantity of cocaine at a time is to tape sixteen one-ounce packets of the powder to any of the following areas:

1. ARMS—Beneath a heavy or loose shirt
2. LEGS—Under loose fitting pants
3. INNER THIGHS—Under loose clothing
4. ANKLES—Behind socks and shoes
5. In the small and middle areas of the back

This method is sometimes used for commercial airline travel, and the packets remain on the body packer throughout his trip until he arrives at a safe location to remove them.

CHAPTER 13

ORGANIZED CRIME

THIS CHAPTER will address a dimension of criminal activity that law enforcement generally considers to be one of the most significant threats to our society today. Generally speaking the precise definition of organized crime varies from source to source, but the National Organized Crime Planning Counsel defines it as "those self perpetuating, structured and disciplined associations of individuals or groups, combined together or in part by illegal means, while protecting their activities through a pattern of graft and corruption."

Traditionally, the term "organized crime" was associated almost exclusively with the Mafia, also known as "la Cosa Nostra." Although the Mafia certainly is an example of organized crime, many other high-level organized crime organizations operate quite freely from its dominance and control, as we will discuss later on in this chapter. In turn, there are many smaller organized crime groups involved in numerous criminal endeavors but are still considered significant law enforcement problems.

These groups may be anything from a ring of shoplifters to the international criminal enterprises of the Italian Mafia, and everything in between. Obviously, the larger the group is and the more resources at its disposal, the greater threat it presents to society. Probably the biggest threat posed by these groups is that they tend to infiltrate all stratas of society, making detection difficult for law enforcement.

These groups are commonly involved in the lucrative drug trade due to its huge profit margin and vast international sources of supply. Depending on the group, many OC organizations already have a distribution network within their organization due to an international membership.

THE MAFIA

Before discussing the Mafia's involvement in the illicit drug trade, let's first review the beginnings of this significant organized crime group.

The spawning of this dangerous organization goes back hundreds of years when ancient Sicily was in the clutches of political, economic, and social repression from foreign conquerors. After the unification of Italy in 1860, Sicilians saw little change. Instead of repression from foreign rulers, they were repressed by the rule and the authority of the Italians from the North.

At the time, the only source of loyalty and trust in which Sicilians could rely was that of "famigila," or blood of my blood. This developed into a philosophy which included non-cooperation with authorities, self-control in the face of adversity, and the "vendetta." The vendetta simply meant that any offense against the famigila was to be avenged regardless of the consequences or how long it took.

The Mafia came to the United States in the late 1800s. Mixed in with other immigrants, few mafioso found opportunities in the United States for traditional jobs. These immigrants huddled together in the "little Italy's" of New York, New Orleans and many other cities across the country. With little legitimate power and little reason to respect political authority, many immigrants turned to illegal occupations and life-styles. Little by little, the forces and influences of today's Mafia began to see its rise to power.

Law enforcement in the United States was somewhat reluctant to identify the Mafia as a significant criminal force until after Prohibition was enacted. The passing of Prohibition in 1920 only served to provide organized crime a vehicle with which to finance itself and gain influence through political and social corruption. Today, the Mafia is believed to have gangs or "families" located in almost every major city throughout the United States. Within this territory, they exercise extreme influence over all major criminal activity.

Though initially reluctant to involve itself with the business of drug smuggling and trafficking, the Mafia was drawn to the enormous profit potential and has now become one of the largest importers of controlled substances in the world. Although actively involved with the smuggling of cocaine, the Mafia's chief drug involvement is with heroin.

During the 1960s, the Mafia fought a bitter war over control of the drug trade with the blacks in Harlem. There are now five Mafia families in New York alone, which control about $45 billion in illicit drugs annually. The American Mafia works closely with the Sicilian Mafia in arranging the shipments of raw opium materials from the "Golden Crescent" to final processing labs in Sicily. Out of the estimated nine thousand pounds of heroin smuggled into the United States each year, it is estimated that at least half is Mafia related.

The Mafia families are highly structured with varying levels of command and authority. Basically, the command structure is as outlined below:

The Boss. He is usually an older member of the organization who maintains family order and concerns himself with the overall profit margin of the family.

The Underboss. This is a member who works under the boss and is directly responsible for keeping the boss informed of any information that is considered important to the organization. He also takes charge of the organization in the event that the boss is absent.

The Lieutenants (Caporegima). These are individuals who are in charge of the soldiers and serve as a buffer between the bosses and the low-level workers.

The Soldiers (Soldati). Also referred to as buttonmen, they are considered to be the lowest level of service within the Mafia. Soldiers may be involved in a particular type of criminal activity, such as drug dealing, bookmaking, and arson, and answer to the lieutenants.

In order to insulate the bosses from the police, the soldiers generally are not permitted to communicate with the upper levels of the family. Often, they are paid a commission for their involvement with certain crimes. Soldiers might also exchange a percentage of their profits with the lieutenants for permission to operate.

The Mafia has extensive involvement in both illegal and legitimate business, reaping huge profits from each. Some legitimate enterprises include:

Nightclubs
Taverns
Restaurants
Garbage Disposal
Real Estate
Labor Unions
The Garment Industry
Vending Machine Companies

Their illicit endeavors include criminal activity in the following areas:

Drug Trafficking/Smuggling
Extortion
Gambling
Loansharking
Alcohol
Labor Racketeering

Aside from the profits derived from legitimate and illicit business enterprises, the Mafia is also actively involved in crimes of violence designed to intimidate those who might consider turning against the organization. Murder and assault are typically used to serve as public affirmations to the power of this dangerous public adversary.

OUTLAW MOTORCYCLE GANGS

Outlaw motorcycle gangs have been a thorn in the side of society for decades, but only recently have these criminal groups been considered or even associated with traditional organized crime. These gangs represent a significant threat to the safety of any community. Though they seem to be nothing more than troublemakers on motorcycles, they have emerged as one of society's most threatening and highly structured organized crime organizations. The federal government has recently documented affiliations between motorcycle gangs and the Mafia, specifically how these gangs have been hired to carry out much of the mob's "dirty work." Strong drug-trafficking links have been uncovered, for instance, between the Hell's Angels chapter in New York and nightclubs owned and operated by the Gambino organized crime family. Similar associations are now documented between the Hell's Angels and known organized crime groups in Cleveland, Pittsburg, and Chicago.

These gangs are considered expansionists, involved in virtually every conceivable criminal activity, devoted to maximizing their profits through their criminal endeavors. The direct association between bikers and involvement in the profitable drug business has long been established. With regard to such dangerous drugs as methamphetamine, amphetamine, and PCP, these gangs are notorious for involvement in their production as well as distribution. Three primary reasons exist that might explain the extensive involvement of these gangs with drug trafficking and manufacturing operations. They are listed as follows:

1. Any drug-trafficking activity which can be conducted entirely within the organization provides increased security for the operation.
2. Being a self-contained operation, the gang does not need to be concerned about competition.
3. The internal distribution network provides for an increased profit margin for the club.

Typically, these groups are somewhat difficult for police to penetrate with undercover agents because of the extensive criminal involvement required of each member. Inroads have been made, however, with the help of police informants who are already on the inside as members or "patch holders."

There are currently more than 850 identified outlaw motorcycle gangs operating in the United States and Canada, ranging from single-chapter gangs with five to ten members, to gangs such as the Hell's Angels with worldwide membership. The following details the origin and development of such gangs.

The story begins in 1946 when the American Motorcycle Association (AMA) sponsored a fourth of July weekend dirt hill climb for motorcycle enthusiasts. Attending this event were hundreds of spectators and contestants, as well as a renegade motorcycle club called the "Pissed-Off Bastards of Bloomington." The gang, made up primarily of ex-GI's and self-professed outcasts, proceeded to disrupt the events by starting fights with spectators. This activity resulted in the arrest of one of the POBOB members by the Holister police. Outraged by this police action, the POBOB club merged on the courthouse and demanded the release of their arrested member.

The media proceeded to get considerable mileage out of this event and created much adverse national publicity for motorcyclists in general. Shortly after the Holister incident, the AMA, in defense, came out with a disclaimer by saying that most motorcycle riders were decent, law-abiding citizens unworthy of any bad publicity. They further stated that in their opinion, 99 percent of all motorcycle riders were not outlaws, and that only the remaining 1 percent were.

The POBOB club, which later became the Hell's Angels, perceived this as a tribute to their uniqueness and have since identified themselves with the symbol, 1%. The Hell's Angels grew in numbers and formed chapters throughout the United States, Canada, and other parts of the world. Other outlaw gangs later formed and claimed to be 1%ers, also. To date there are four major outlaw motorcycle gangs, all of which don the 1% image:

The Hell's Angels (approximately 1,200 members in U.S. and Canada)
The Outlaws (approximately 1,500 members)
The Banditos (approximately 400 members)
The Pagans (approximately 1,000 members)

These four groups have chapters in various areas throughout the United States claiming specific areas of operation or "turfs." It is common for these groups to fight over territorial rights; for example, the Hell's Angels and the Outlaws have been at war for quite some time (Figs. 19–22).

With control over an estimated 40 percent of the entire methamphetamine and amphetamine market in the United States, these clubs also dedicate their existence to violent anti-social behavior and a life-style considered appalling to most decent law-abiding citizens.

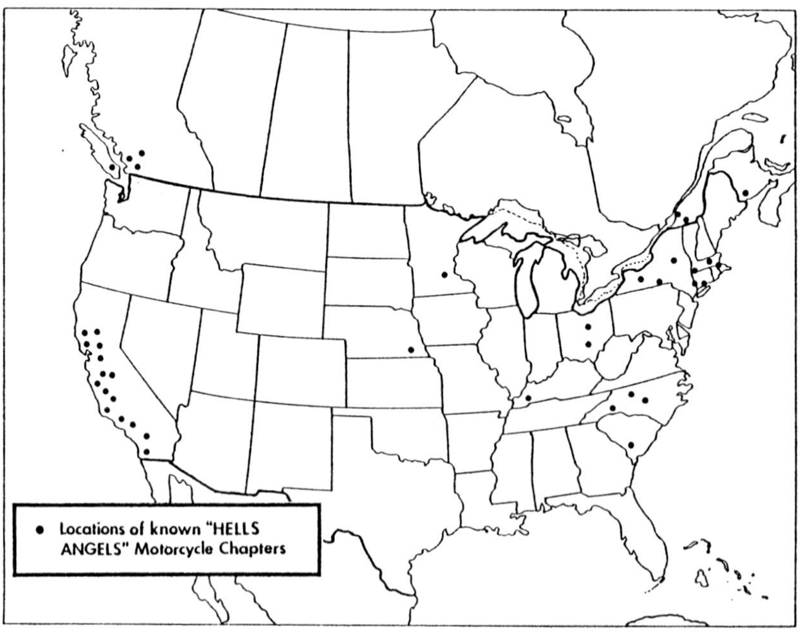

Figure 19. Map of the United States—Hell's Angels chapters.

Figure 20. Map of the United States—Outlaws chapters.

Figure 21. Map of the United States—Banditos chapters.

Figure 22. Map of the United States—Pagans chapters.

Figure 23. The Hell's Angels motorcycle gang has chapters all over the world, and members frequently meet during "runs" and discuss club business. (Photo courtesy of the U.S. Marshal's Service.)

Involvement in the drug trade is probably the most common criminal activity pursued by these gangs. As mentioned, motorcycle gangs have been particularly successful in asserting control over the methamphetamine drug market in the United States and Canada. Furthermore, they are a likely conduit between drug manufacturers and street dealers, and, because of their sworn code of honor, they are extremely difficult to penetrate by police agents. The degree of violence displayed by these clubs usually deters efforts to restrict market entry and reinforces a monopoly of distribution in areas throughout the country (Fig. 23).

Aside from the four major 1% clubs throughout the country, many other motorcycle gangs exist and may consider themselves to be 1%ers. These clubs are referred to as "independent" motorcycle gangs and, though still dangerous, are usually much smaller in size and usually operate with the permission of the larger club in the area. Examples of a few independent motorcycle gangs in the United States are as follows:

The Dirty Dozen—Arizona
The Gypsy Jokers—The Pacific Northwest
The Sons of Silence—Colorado
The Vagos—Southern California, Oregon, Texas
The Warlocks—Pennsylvania, New Jersey, Delaware

Although outlaw motorcycle gangs exist in a cloak of secrecy, recent arrests, resulting in the seizure of club records and documents, have provided law enforcement with significant information regarding club structure, rules, and bylaws. The following sections provide a breakdown of some of the provisions within the internal structure of an outlaw motorcycle club.

Gang Structure

Outlaw motorcycle gangs are highly structured and have a rank and file similar to that of a paramilitary operation. Here are some of the positions held within a 1% club:

The National President. This individual is usually the leader and founder of the club and is constantly surrounded by other gang members who serve him as bodyguards or "enforcers" of his decisions. He will make the final decisions on matters that are disputed by fellow members and on issues that concern the club in general.

The Regional Representative. Also known as the vice-president of the club, he is in charge of club business in specially designated regions.

The matters in which the regional representative become involved with do not require input from the national president and usually deal with problems on a local level.

The National Secretary. For the most part, this position is that of club treasurer. The treasurer is responsible for handling the club's money and for collecting dues from members.

The National Enforcer. This individual answers only to the national president and acts as a personal bodyguard as well as an enforcer of the club's bylaws. He is also known to be responsible for injuries and even killings of other club members who are considered problems or threats to the organization.

The Chapter President. Those in this position are usually elected into office by members or those who are strong in personality or physical strength. The chapter president has authority over chapter business.

The Vice-President. This position is second in command to chapter president and usually takes over in the president's absence.

The Chapter Secretary. Just as the national secretary handles the club's money on a national level, the chapter secretary is in charge of the local chapter's money.

Sergeant at Arms. Due to the violent and unruly nature of outlaw motorcycle gangs, the sergeant at arms provides order during rallies and meetings. He is often the member with the most physical strength and must be absolutely loyal to the president.

The Road Captain. The road captain is in charge of the logistics of certain club activities or outings. He maps out the routes that will be traveled, makes arrangements for food and fuel, and plans for scheduled maintenance stops. He might also carry the club's money and use it for bail if necessary.

Regular members of the club are accepted members who have undergone a probationary period lasting anywhere from one month to a year. The members, also known as "patch holders," must pay their dues, swear to live by the bylaws of the club, and always carry out the decisions of the president. As previously mentioned, potential members must become probates before they are accepted as regular members of the organization. They must also be sponsored by a regular member and, during the probationary period, must prove their worthiness as a member by doing whatever they are told.

It is typical for a probate to be required to commit a felony to prove to fellow members that he is not an undercover police officer. Probates are often required to carry weapons or drugs for regular members and to stand guard during club parties. They will not be issued a club patch or "colors" until they receive a unanimous vote from the club.

Other types of members are unofficial or "honorary" members. These members are not required to undergo a probationary period, but they are not allowed to vote on club issues. An honorary member can be anyone such as an attorney or a motorcycle mechanic who has provided a service for the club.

All organized outlaw gangs have their own rules or "charter," dictating the club's structure and the members' standards of behavior. Even though these bylaws may differ from club to club, they all govern matters such as:

- Membership requirements
- Accepted behavior during trips
- Punishments for violating the charter

Specific examples of club rules or bylaws are as follows:

- No member may transfer from one chapter to another without approval from the chapter president.
- All members must be over 18 years old.
- All prospective members must be sponsored by a regular member.
- All members must pay monthly dues.
- All prospective members must complete a probationary period.

Other violations considered more severe, and dealt with accordingly, are stealing from club members, talking to the police, striking a brother biker, being dishonest in any drug deals with other members, and surprisingly, using drugs by injection.

Gang members possess tattoos which investigating officers must examine carefully and document. These markings may provide police with information as to a biker's "handle" (nick-name) and other identifying data such as a prison which he had served in time. It is important to note that most bikers prefer to use their handles rather than their actual names to help insulate themselves from the police. These handles might be names such as "EZ," "Bear," "Pan Head," "Squirrel," and are often tatooed somewhere on their body. The basic biker philosophy of the 1% outlaw gang is also frequently tattooed on them or worn on their clothing in the form of patches with the following initials:

FTW—Fuck The World
GFOD—God Forgives, Outlaws Don't
GFAD—God Forgives, Angels Don't
SOOOF—Stay Out Of Our Face

These slogans have the shock value commonly sought by such criminals. Their honor code of "an eye for an eye" is strictly enforced. One must always remember that outlaw motorcycle gangs strive to be hated and feared and will always go out of their way to appall society with their actions and mannerisms.

After his colors, a biker's second priority is his motorcycle, to which he will show more care and attention than his wife or girl friend. A third priority is his dog—these guys always have dogs—or his woman, also called mamas, sheep, or old ladies.

Outlaw motorcycle gang members are not only white supremacists but male chauvinists as well, so a woman will frequently be sold, given away, or traded before a biker risks the loss of a dog or motorcycle. The final priority to a 1%er is living by the motto: "What's mine is yours, what's yours is mine." Bikers have no qualms about using another member's wife, girl friend, motorcycle, house, anything.

These unique types of organized crime figures continue to pose growing threats and problems for society and the law enforcement community. The controlling of crime by these threatening groups is, however, a realistic goal with the use of diligent law enforcement strategies and inventive criminal laws.

PRISON GANGS

Another form of organized crime that has just recently been studied is that of organized prison gangs operating within the penitentiaries in the United States. With extensive involvement in a multitude of criminal activity including murder, extortion, and drug traffic, this organized crime group has established a foothold in the overall American crime picture.

These organizations, originally established and structured within the walls of prison institutions, take on a militant and revolutionary stance against law enforcement in general. Hardened criminals are often aligned with known revolutionary extremists, and, while their goals may vary from one gang to the next, they are basically a recruiting ground for organized crime groups in the United States.

The original cause and purpose for this type of gang is born out of traditional prison violence and offers, on an individual basis, protection and a sense of belonging for its members. Those prospective members desiring permanent membership must prove their worth to already established members. The mutual protection offered each member is from the frequent incidents of prison rape, extortion, theft, and accompanying acts of violence that are often uncontrollable and unreported by prison guards and corrections authorities.

Gang structure may vary, but usually upon acceptance members must be willing to commit any crime that gang leaders request of them, including murder. This will prove gang loyalty and dedication. The associations made as members of these gangs are usually maintained even after one or more members have been paroled out of prison. Typically, these ex-cons perform criminal activities on the outside of the prison walls to further the illegal enterprises within the walls, such as drug trafficking and penal smuggling of drugs, weapons, money, and other contraband. These criminal activities provide financial support for the goals of the prison gang.

Many prison gangs throughout the country are generally well acquainted with the structure and reputation of other rival gangs located in different states. Exhibiting a desire to be the dominant gang, many of these organizations use methods of intimidation to gain recognition within the country's prison network.

The California prison system has several significant prison gangs which operate throughout the state. These gangs have considerable influence on criminal activity occurring within as well as outside the prison walls.

The Mexican Mafia (EME). This is a prison gang that dates back to 1957 and was originally comprised of a small group of Mexican-American inmates from the Los Angeles area. In 1966 they moved their operation out into the free society, at which time a chain of command was structured for its members. The EME then grew in numbers and began to foster respect from other inmates until 1967, when the gang supposedly committed its first murder, which was drug related. The victim was another gang member who was allegedly talking to the police (see Chapter 14, "Drug-Related Crime").

The EME is considered the most powerful prison gang in California and operates both inside and outside of prison. The gang is also believed to have significant drug-trafficking connections in Mexico, South

America, and Europe and supposedly owns a ranch house in Mexico that serves as a hideout and base station for the gang.

One of the primary methods of operation of the gang is to take over drug trafficking in any given area. This is done by an EME member contacting a local drug dealer in a neighborhood and advising him that, as of that moment, he will be doing business with the EME. If the dealer refuses, the EME sends forces to beat or even kill the dealer. After this occurs, the EME then proceeds to set up business in the area itself.

Nuestra Familia (NF). This group is not quite as large as the Mexican Mafia but appears to be better organized. The NF still stands as the Mexican Mafia's biggest foe and is comprised of Latins, Indians, and a few Caucasians. The leader of the NF holds rank as the "General" and has total and absolute power over the gang and its members. Other members also hold rank within the organization with positions such as captain and lieutenant. The achievement of rank is usually based on the number of murders or "hits" a member is involved in.

The NF originally began as a prison protection gang from the EME but now has spread to the free society (as the EME) and, accordingly, is heavily involved in drug trafficking.

The Texas Syndicate. Even though it is the most recent prison gang to become organized, the Texas Syndicate is the gang most feared by all of the prison gangs in California. Made up entirely of Mexican-American members mainly from the El Paso area, its membership is estimated at seventy-five official members, with up to five hundred members within the prison system. This gang operates heavily in Bakersfield and San Jose, California, as well as El Paso and San Antonio, Texas. The Texas Syndicate has established its ultimate goal as gaining total control of drug traffic within their areas of operation.

The Arayan Brotherhood. The beginning of the Arayan Brotherhood can be traced back to the early 1960s when it got its start in San Quentin. This group is an all white group that commonly focuses aggression against black inmates. Due to the drug-trafficking wars between these prison gangs, the Arayan Brotherhood recently signed an alliance with the EME to fight against the NF. This agreement has since opened up some new sources for the gangs, as well as provided new outlets for distribution.

Many other prison gangs exist and maintain some of the same goals as the four major gangs just discussed. Some of these groups are listed as follows:

The United Prisoners Union
The Black Muslims or Nation of Islam (NOI)
The Black Guerrilla Family—BGF
The Black Liberation Army—BLA
Us or Us Incorporated
The Polar Bear Party
Venceremos Brigade
Venceremos Organization

It is important to point out that many prison gangs, such as those discussed earlier, were originally established within prison but expanded to the free society. Conversely, gangs operating in the streets are often reorganized in prisons after members are convicted of crimes and continue to operate quite freely within the prison environment.

Listed below are street organizations which have a tendency to operate both in and out of prisons:

THE WEATHERMEN. Considered a violent revolutionary organization in existence since 1969 and heavily involved with bombings and related terrorist activities.

CHINESE GANGS. The two primary Chinese gangs are known as the Fong Gang and the Wah Chings. These gangs pose a significant threat to areas such as San Francisco, Portland, Chicago and New York City.

CRIPS. These are neighborhood gangs operating between Los Angeles and San Francisco and contain members whose ages range from eleven years old to thirty. These gangs are usually at war with one another and have a total membership of about 5,000 members. These groups are extremely active in drug trafficking and violent street crime such as robberies.

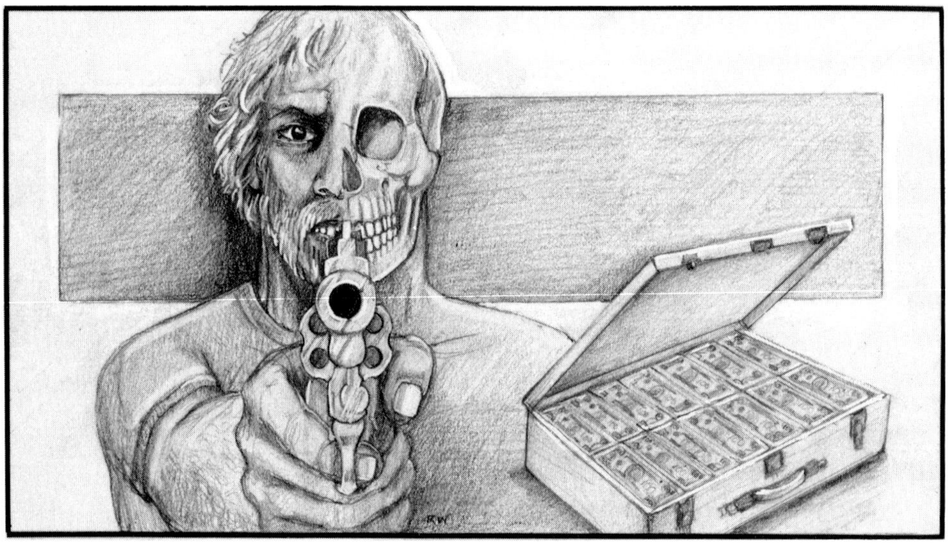

CHAPTER 14

DRUG-RELATED CRIME

IT IS NO secret that a definitive, but complex, correlation exists between drug crimes and other types of crime. However, the nature and extent of the link between drug crimes and other crime are still far from being fully understood, so the term "drug-related crime" remains somewhat general. Law enforcement officials hope to clarify the correlation to better predict drug-trafficking patterns and general criminal involvement.

Although magazines and newspapers commonly sensationalize gangland executions and other so-called drug-related crimes, much of the violence is among different criminal groups desiring control over a portion of the drug market. This activity is not uncommon in most major cities in the United States. For example, in 1981 over 25 percent of all homicides in Dade County, Florida were the result of drug-trafficking groups carrying out machine-gun-style assassinations in public places. Those acts, committed by criminals against criminals, are constantly under study by law enforcement officers and remain a significant component to the overall drug-trafficking picture.

Obviously, drug traffickers run many risks in the manufacture, importation, and distribution of their commodity. Criminals are concerned about security from the police as well as from other criminals wishing to rob, burglarize, or even murder them for their product or cash profits. This explains why most drug raids commonly net the seizure of weapons, explosives, and even booby traps.

Associations between the drug dealer and drug user are usually very exclusive. Each criminal casts suspicion on every new acquaintance and maintains a constant arms length from even his most trusted associates. Trust in the drug world is rare and is commonly acquired by the mutual practice of anti-social behavior and the commission of various street crimes.

With such a high degree of distrust between drug criminals and the endless availability of weapons, the reality of drug-related crime is almost inevitable. The addict population also poses unique law enforcement concerns with regard to crimes against property to get money to purchase drugs. In addressing this problem, law enforcement has attempted to isolate variables which contribute to this criminal activity, such as the level of addiction and the type of addicting drug used by the offender. With considerations to personal and property crimes, the two basic motivations behind drug-related criminal activity are as follows:

1. **Money:** For the purchase of drugs by an addicted person or drug dealer. This is accomplished by committing robberies, burglaries, larceny, or drug rip-offs.

2. **Retribution (violence):** To avenge someone when a problem of an illegal nature arises between two drug suspects. Retaliation might be directed against police informers, those who renege on drug deals, or those who steal from other dealers or competitors. Due to the illegal nature of these situations, the police are not contacted to intervene and the situations are usually violent rather than profit oriented (see Chapter 4, "Profit Margin—The Allure of the Drug Business").

Much evidence during recent years shows the association between drugs and crime and helps to explain how the involvement with drugs contributes to general criminal behavior. The National Institute of Justice reports that in 1983, one-third of all inmates of state prisons were under the influence of some kind of mind-altering substance just before they committed the crimes for which they were incarcerated. This includes illicit drugs as well as alcohol.

In understanding the effects of different drugs, we realize that some substances accelerate the function of the brain and may cause an individual to be more aggressive in his behavior. Conversely, other drugs depress the central nervous system and may reduce the likelihood for criminal involvement.

Studies conducted on drug use and crime reveal data on how many individuals are involved in drug abuse, as well as the total costs of drugs to society, but little information exists on the reasons these criminal types become involved in the first place.

Although it cannot be generalized that all addicts are criminals, it is generally accepted that the level of drug abuse by an individual will most likely reflect his degree of criminal involvement to one extent or another. For example, those who use drugs, such as heroin, in different degrees of severity are likely to be involved in criminal behavior with corresponding degrees of severity.

Predictably, street-level users (in particular those who are addicted) will commit crimes that will afford them enough income to support their drug habit. These crimes will range from robbery, burglary, stealing, drug dealing, prostitution, and many others. The street-level users in this predicament are opportunists rather than professional criminals and might involve themselves in virtually any type of criminal activity for financial gain.

Those addicts who steal for drug money usually only realize about one-fourth the value of the item stolen when sold on the illicit market. It is also unfortunate that many otherwise law-abiding citizens provide a ready market for stolen items such as jewelry, stereo equipment, auto accessories, and expensive clothing. This market provides the addict a constant outlet for stolen property and an incentive to continue in this type of criminal activity.

Aside from the involvement of drug users in different types of crimes, these criminal types are often associated with the use of violence. Recent NIJ studies have revealed that heroin-using offenders are just as likely as their non-drug-using counterparts to commit violent crimes and are even more likely to commit robbery and weapons offenses. In fact, robberies and assaults are proving to be rare among criminally active youths who are not also involved in illicit drug use (Fig. 24).

Drug treatment programs have traditionally attempted to curb drug-related street violence and crime by detoxification programs aimed at drug users. One of the stronger arguments for drug treatment is that, by reducing the taking of hard drugs by addicts, the corresponding level of criminal activity and violence will also be reduced. The implementation of treatment programs, such as methadone maintenance, have proven somewhat effective in this area. This is where methadone (also an addictive drug) is given to addicts in a controlled clinical environment so that the addict will avoid the discomfort of withdrawal and, hopefully, reduce his need to commit crimes to afford his habit.

A recent survey was co-sponsored by the National Institute of Justice and the National Institute of Drug Abuse which examined criminal involvement of 201 Harlem heroin addicts. The New York State Division of Substance Abuse Services gathered data between 1980 and 1982 for this survey and reported information on drug use and how the subjects supported themselves during that period of time.

Figure 24. These Uzi machine guns were seized by drug agents during a 1985 raid on an illicit methamphetamine laboratory in Durant, Oklahoma. (Photo courtesy of the Oklahoma Bureau of Narcotics and Dangerous Drugs.)

Initial findings revealed that the subjects averaged 316 drug sales per year and were involved in an additional 564 drug-dealing-type offenses such as "steering" or directing persons where to buy drugs. Additional findings were that almost all subjects used other drugs in addition to heroin: 90 percent used cocaine and alcohol, and 73 percent used marijuana.

The study further classified these drug users according to their frequency of drug use:

Daily—(six to seven days per week)
Regular—(three to five days per week)
Irregular—(two days or less per week)

The daily heroin users each consumed over $17,000 worth of drugs per year compared to about $5,000 for the "irregular" users. Interestingly enough, the daily users committed about twice as many robberies as regular users and about five times as many as the irregular users. Ironically, though, they did not have a significantly higher arrest rate than the less intensive users. The study concludes that the daily user might be considered a more "successful" criminal, because he commits more crimes and uses more drugs than the less regular user and remains undetected by police more frequently.

Ironically, the income derived from street crimes is surprisingly low for all categories of users. The daily users, for instance, netted an average of $41 per crime, while the irregular users netted an average of $25 per crime. The average returns from robbery and burglary were $80 and $81 per crime, respectively. These figures are quite modest compared to the substantial risks involved in the commission of the crimes themselves.

Aside from street crime, the legitimate business community is also affected by drug-related criminal activity. Not only does a company suffer losses from absenteeism by drug-dependent employees but also from theft within the company by those needing money for drug habits. These thefts are not unique to low-level employees and frequently involve high-ranking management personnel, as well (see Chapter 15, "Drugs in the Workplace").

MONEY LAUNDERING

The engaging of money-laundering activities by high-level drug traffickers has posed a significant threat to ongoing drug-suppression efforts. This has created a new type of criminal who is generally removed from the street and is concerned only with the hiding of illegal drug revenues. It is common that this violator may not be involved with substance abuse at all on a personal level but is only interested in his monetary piece of the pie.

Traditionally, these laundering activities have been somewhat difficult to investigate due to aliases of suspects and fake business names, addresses, phone numbers, and bank accounts. Actually, there are as many ways to launder money as the imagination can fathom.

The primary reasons cash is hidden from authorities are cited below:

1. So it will not be taxed.
2. So it will not be seized or forfeited by law enforcement authorities.
3. So the launderer will not be caught and prosecuted.

Many traffickers have chosen to deposit their illegal money in foreign bank accounts under the belief that they are free from U.S. search-and-seizure authority. This is true, in part, because many countries also have bank secrecy laws that restrict any outside government intervention. It is becoming more common, however, for some countries, such as Switzerland, to assist the U.S. in investigations once a criminal enterprise is identified.

According to a 1983 U.S. Department of Justice training booklet entitled *Investigation and Prosecution of Illegal Money Laundering,* traffickers may typically launder money through countries such as Panama, the Cayman Islands, the Bahamas, and the Netherlands Antilles, all of which have a legal climate optimal for the laundering of "dirty" money. These countries have laws that generally prohibit the disclosure of any information about their customers' accounts.

The tool most frequently used by drug enforcement agencies against money-laundering activities is the Bank Secrecy Act (BSA), contained in Titles 31 and 12 of the United States Code. This federal act became law in 1970 and has proven to be one of the more effective laws in combatting this complicated enforcement priority. What the Bank Secrecy Act effectively does is create a paper trail for investigators. This enables the tracing of drug and other proceeds back to their illegal source and helps to identify persons involved, money, and other assets acquired through illegal activities.

The BSA requires that any transaction involving cash or equivalent at financial institutions exceeding $10,000 must be reported by the institution to the federal government. This also applies to currency taken out or brought into the country. Most drug dealers shy away from this requirement, because they are generally touchy about their names appearing in government reports.

Many financial institutions where such currency is deposited exist only on paper as a ploy to evade detection by authorities. The BSA law, however, broadly defines "financial institution" to include individuals as well as banks. Because of this broad definition, "persons" who receive amounts of currency exceeding the specified amount will also be required to file currency transaction reports.

Money-laundering investigations examine the following types of financial transactions:

1. Checking account records
2. Savings account records
3. Negotiated checks, exchange instruments
4. Cashier's checks and traveler's checks
5. Telegraphic transfers, deposit tickets
6. Credit card records

It is believed that one of the best starting points for investigating large organized crime operations is to start at their financial base. The BSA provides law enforcement this ability, but it should also be used in harmony with other drug enforcement laws such as RICO, conspiracy, and wiretap laws (see Chapter 8, "The Drug Laws—The Narc's Toolbox").

Part IV

DRUGS AS A SOCIAL DISEASE

WITH ALL OF the different philosophies on how to rid drug-dependent persons from the clutches of addiction and how to convince potential drug users of the dangers of drugs, concerned persons have numerous options available to them. These options vary from drug-prevention programs involving classroom drug education, brochures, films, and counseling to treatment programs requiring possible hospital admittance and major medical attention.

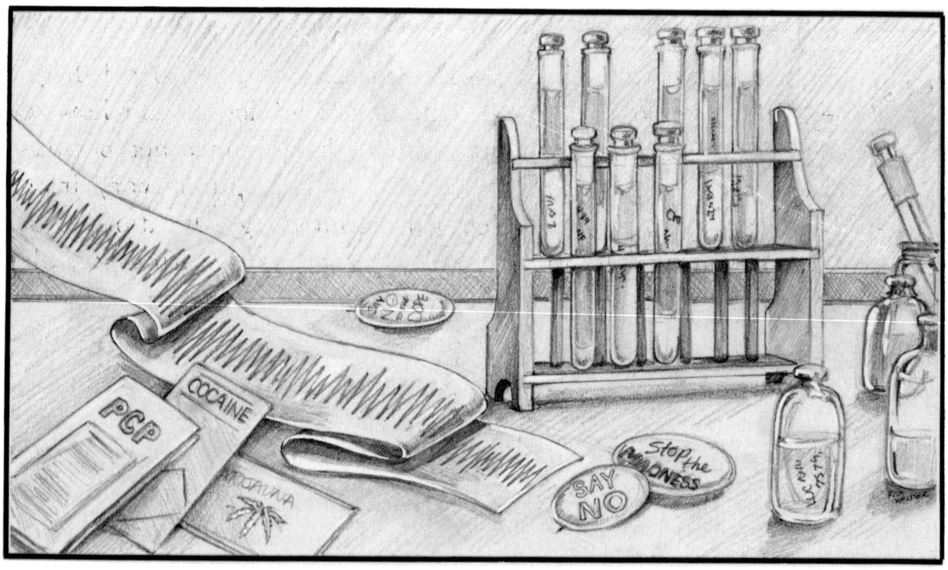
PCP
COCAINE
SAY NO
Stop the

CHAPTER 15

DRUGS IN THE WORKPLACE

MUCH HAS BEEN written in recent months about the effects of drug usage in the workplace. According to some estimates, it cost American industry as much as $100 billion in 1986, compared to an estimated $60 billion in 1983.

As one can imagine, dealing with employee drug use can be an extremely complex issue, with concerns for both the employee and his employer. The National Institute of Drug Abuse estimates that 44 percent of the nation's work force had taken illicit drugs during 1985. Victims of this harsh reality are not only the drug users themselves but their employers and fellow co-workers. Prime candidates for drug abuse on the job are doctors, lawyers, secretaries, and truck drivers, as well as those working two jobs or jobs requiring excessive overtime.

Drug abuse statistics have shown that more people are using drugs on the job than ever, and now more cocaine is used than traditionally preferred marijuana. There are a number of reasons for this, aside from the trendy association users have with cocaine. First, cocaine is much more easily concealed than marijuana and when used it does not give off the distinctive odor of "pot." This means that a user could conceivably consume quantities of cocaine almost anywhere in and around the workplace and still avoid detection by co-workers or supervisors.

For the most part, though, cocaine typically provides the user with a feeling of confidence while working and a sense of motivation. When taking the drug, users not only feel good about themselves and the job they are doing, they feel more readily accepted by their co-workers. In comparison, marijuana use has subsided in recent years, primarily because marijuana tends to act as a mild depressant, actually slowing down user activity and stifling personal motivation.

Factors contributing to general drug use on the job are many, but a large percentage of the activity could very well be attributed to old-fashioned peer pressure, which for many people is as intense in adulthood as in early adolescence. Another reason is directly associated with the amount of boredom an employee experiences in his daily work tasks. Here, drugs offer an escape from the monotony of a routine work environment, such as an auto assembly line.

However, some people working in fast-paced jobs also abuse drugs on the job due to a desire to keep up with the demands of a high-pressure position. Those in this circumstance frequently offer fellow workers and clients drugs as a social icebreaker or as a friendly introduction to a hopeful business relationship.

Recent studies show that employees who use drugs are considerably less productive than those who do not and tend to miss up to ten times as much work. Furthermore, users are three times more likely to have on-the-job accidents than those who abstain from drug use.

Aside from the psychological and physiological dangers, drug use in the workplace tends to breed other work-related problems, such as injuries, internal theft, and poor work-related decisions.

The concern is greatest, however, when the loss of life is at risk due to accidents and mistakes. During the last ten years numerous deaths resulting from auto, train, and aircraft accidents have been blamed on employees using drugs on the job.

The federal government is concerned not only about inefficiency, absenteeism and a tendency toward accidents resulting from drug use but also about slipups with confidential material. For example, an employee on the job requiring a high security clearance might sell or compromise classified information for drugs or money. Imagine also the potential disaster resulting from a drug-related accident on a missile site.

Evidence of drug use in many white-collar jobs is also more commonplace. This is true for low-level workers as well as individuals in upper-management positions. Many executives for large companies prefer to think of drug use on the job as relating only to the assembly line and not to upper management.

In an effort to help combat the problem of drug use on the job, many companies are resorting to the planting of undercover agents and covert surveillance equipment to observe locker rooms, break rooms, parking lots, and even local taverns frequented by employees. Other measures considered less dramatic involve the implementation of drug abuse programs to help employees who have acknowledged their drug habits.

According to the National Institute of Justice, about 25 percent of the Fortune 500's largest companies have established in-house employee assistance programs. Many of these programs were originally established for alcohol abuse but now have been expanded to deal with illicit drug abuse. These companies believe that it is more cost effective to try and help someone who has been a long time employee than to hire and train new employees. According to a March 17, 1986, issue of *Time* magazine, in-house drug treatment programs are becoming more and more common. Following are the highlights of the in-house drug treatment program used by Mobil Oil Company:

1. Employees with a drug problem can stop by any of a number of medical facilities offered by the company. A supervisor may also be given the prerogative to recommend that the employee be examined.
2. After the initial examination or treatment, the employee is then referred to a hospital's outpatient drug clinic for extended treatment that lasts from four to six weeks.
3. During the treatment periods, the patient is given sick leave with pay and his/her status is kept confidential.
4. The cost of the treatment program is covered by the patient's employee benefit package.
5. Once the employee returns to the job, he/she is allowed to attend follow-up visits on company time.

DRUG TESTING

In 1986, President Reagan voluntarily submitted to a urine test for drugs before requiring all seventy-eight White House employees to do the same. Many companies consider the testing of employees for drugs, while other companies fear that it might be an invasion of their employees' personal rights.

A critical balance must always be maintained when weighing reasonable expectations of privacy and confidentiality against principles of performance, productivity, and public safety. The primary reason for drug testing is to weed out candidates for employment that might have an existing drug problem, as well as identify drug-dependent employees already on the job.

Generally speaking, it is the policy of most employers not to hire applicants whose urine tests positive for the use of illicit substances. The advocates of these types of programs have an important point in their favor: they work!

From a traditional standpoint, the medical examination of potential employees to determine their fitness for a job is a long-standing policy with many employers. Only recently, however, has this hiring practice been expanded to include drug use detection.

Many companies boast of the benefits of such a program. For instance, companies such as the Georgia Power Company and Southern Pacific Railway have seen job-related accidents drop by a minimum of 70 percent each. The Navy boasts that drug use in the ranks has been reduced from 48 percent to 4 percent since employee drug testing was implemented.

Some of the larger companies that have employee-assistance programs are Exxon, IBM, Federal Express, United Airlines, TWA airlines, AT&T, and the *New York Times.*

At the time of the writing of this text, no federal or state law directly prohibits the use of drug-detection programs. Part of the controversy surrounding drug testing is that employers who require employees to take the tests may hold it against the employees if they refuse. Opponents of drug-testing programs claim that employees who refuse are unjustly considered guilty until proven innocent. Furthermore, it is thought that forcing an unwilling employee to take a test that could produce evidence against them is, very likely, a violation of their Fourth and Fifth Amendment rights.

Some recent court rulings say that individuals do not waive their constitutional rights when accepting federal employment, and that nothing in civil service can require an employee to do so. Other legal opinions say that given "reasonable suspicion" of drug use is enough to warrant testing of an employee. It would be sad to think, for example, that an air traffic controller suspected of being high on the job could not be tested for drugs because of his employer's fear of civil liability.

Generally speaking, however, employers should always use common sense when administering urine screening tests to minimize possible future legal challenges by employees.

The cost and reliability factors of drug tests are common considerations for employers wishing to implement drug-testing programs. The costs of drug-screening tests, however, are not as prohibitive as they once were. For example, the reagents for drug testing by the Washington D.C. Pretrial Services Agency averaged seven dollars per sample in 1985, while the quality of testing in general is considered extremely reliable.

The issue of reliability was a valid one in 1984 when the United States Air Force had to reinstate 6,500 airmen who were dismissed due to improperly administered tests. It is possible, with some tests, for a false positive reading to show up. Certain cold capsules may give a false reading for amphetamines, for instance. If the test itself is valid, mix-ups can be avoided if a chain of custody is strictly enforced by all essential laboratory personnel.

THE URINE TEST

The urine test in employee-assistance programs is one of the most common methods of drug detection in the workplace. Used by employers more and more, many companies have developed both pre-employment and in-service drug-screening programs to help protect the health and safety of all employees. To date, this practice of drug screening, along with programs of treatment, prevention, and drug education, is proving to be an effective way of managing substance abuse in industry.

The frequency with which companies should screen their employees should depend on the risk factors associated with safety, security, and health. These testing procedures have evolved over the past two years, ranging from post-accident screening to random, spur-of-the-moment testing. It should be noted, however, that the testing of employees for drugs shows only that the subject has ingested an illicit substance, not that he is mentally impaired on the job.

The two primary methods of drug screening are the EMIT (Enzyme Multiplied Immunoassay Test) system, distributed by the Syva Company, and the Abuscreen system, distributed by Roche Diagnostics, both of which are based on immunoassay techniques. According to the National Institute of Justice, the EMIT test is considered the most common test used in employee testing programs, and the Syva Company boasts a 97 percent accuracy rate in its use. EMIT is a semiautomated system with three basic components:

1. A carousal automatically measures the reagents (the chemicals) that are added to the sample to perform the test. It then pumps the solution into the second component, the spectrophotometer.

2. The spectrophotometer reads the absorption of light waves through a standard amount of reagent-urine sample. A numerical value is thus generated representing the presence or absence of an illegal substance in each sample. This test does not measure the amount of the substance in the urine, only its presence or absence.
3. A computer is used as the third component to print out a hard copy of the test results.

The Syva Company offers a two-day training program for administration of the test and machines. The EMIT system can process up to sixty-five tests per hour, using machines that clean themselves between each test. These machines are also calibrated several times throughout the day for accuracy.

Regardless of the testing procedure used, if an initial screening assay indicates a sample as being positive, a second assay should then be performed on the sample for confirmation. A confirmation assay is considered to be more reliable than a simple screening assay.

These tests are commonly used with the help of gas chromatography (GC) and gas chromatography/mass spectrometry. These are extremely sophisticated methods that require highly trained technicians to administer them. Both the mass spectrometer and the gas chromatograph are commonly used by chemists in the identification of drugs purchased by undercover agents on the street, and the reliability of these instruments is usually unquestioned by defense attorneys in court proceedings.

Finally, there is yet another type of drug test which is currently being considered as an alternative for EMIT. This is the testing of a subject's hair for evidence of past drug use.

Time magazine reported in 1986 that a Los Angeles chemist name Werner Baumgartner had developed a testing method that uses radiation. This test, considered more reliable than urine testing, reveals not only what drug has been taken but when it was taken as well.

CHAPTER 16

TREATMENT AND PREVENTION

DRUG TREATMENT

TREATMENT philosophies for drug-dependent persons vary according to the specific drugs of dependence. Some treatments focus on psychological conditions, while other treatments focus on physiological conditions. Involuntary treatment programs offer choices for the drug-dependent person, while some programs are court ordered and do not require the patient's consent. In programs such as this, an individual may be required to start treatment, continue it, or both. Ambulatory treatment is where the patient visits a treatment program on an outpatient basis at different intervals. Many programs currently exist throughout the country offering treatment based on this concept. Detoxification programs, however, handle only those who are physically addicted, and attempt to rid the patient of his physical craving for the drug. For the most part, however, it is the psychological dependency which is considered to be more difficult to manage than physical dependency, which is why so many different types of treatment programs exist.

For example, heroin addicts are frequently influenced by their environment, so an ideal treatment program is a therapeutic community, removing them from the pressures of street life. Some alcoholics, however, find social relations stressful and might prefer a group therapy environment for treatment.

For the most part, patients in long-term programs participate in a number of levels of care. Typically, the highest degree of therapy is implemented at the entry level of the program and is subsequently reduced throughout the treatment process.

This portion of the chapter will attempt to identify and discuss the various types of treatment programs available to the drug-dependent individual that are recognized by the Harvard School of Public Health.

Acute-Care Hospital Programs

Acute-care hospital programs are those which offer the drug-dependent person optimum medical care and attention. Usually offered by larger hospital facilities, these programs provide the following levels of treatment:

1. An evaluation of the patient's psychological and physiological posture through a series of diagnostic tests.
2. Stabilizing of the patient's condition.
3. A safe, medically approved withdrawal process.
4. An educational process where the patient understands the seriousness of his condition.
5. Reasons to continue treatment.

Programs such as these usually last from three to thirty days and are designed to custom fit each patient's individual requirements. Throughout the program, many physical and psychological tests are administered, including blood and urine examinations.

Acute hospital treatment programs are usually expensive due to the medical expertise required by each patient. Specialists such as psychiatrists, psychologists, physicians, registered nurses, social workers, and counselors boost the overall cost to a possible $10,000 for a three-week program.

Residential Programs

Rehabilitation programs focus primarily on education and therapy. The cost of this program is usually lower than that of acute-care programs, because fewer medical personnel and fewer medical facilities are needed. There is, however, a greater need for mental health workers and counselors.

Residential treatment programs are especially beneficial if the drug-dependent person finds it difficult to stay drug free due to lack of employer or family support. The various types of residential programs are discussed below:

Hospital-Based Programs. These are usually administered by hospitals and may last up to one month. The program is highly structured and offers basically the same abstinence-oriented treatment to all who enter. The program parallels other programs such as Alcoholics Anonymous and Narcotics Anonymous.

Freestanding Facilities. This program, based outside a hospital, is usually not recommended for severely addicted persons. What the program does offer is a pleasant recreational setting for the drug-dependent person. The stay at a freestanding facility is typically longer than thirty days and involves professional personnel such as psychologists, counselors, and social workers.

Therapeutic Communities. These programs gained popularity in the 1950s in rehabilitating hard-core drug addicts. Operating within a highly structured environment, personnel in this program try to reshape the personality and behavior patterns of the drug-dependent person. In this setting, the patients provide support for each other and contribute to daily maintenance of the treatment facility.

The program is considered relatively successful and, because it is usually state supported, drug addicts may receive counseling or other treatment for free.

Detoxification Units

These facilities provide the subject food, shelter, and counseling and are usually sponsored by charity organizations such as the Salvation Army. The drug-dependent person only stays from one to three days and is offered a chance to get straight before returning to the street.

Partial Hospital Programs

This intermediate level of treatment is for those who require more than just one or two days of care but are not severely impaired. The program is offered in either afternoon or evening blocks. Educational films and learning materials as well as peer group support are essential to this program.

Outpatient Care Programs

Outpatient care programs are usually offered as an alternative to residential programs. Although design and quality varies, the programs frequently center around a group setting including former patients who offer support.

Other examples of outpatient care programs are methadone maintenance centers, educational seminars, counseling, and group therapy.

DRUG PREVENTION

According to the National Institute of Drug Abuse, in 1960 less than 1 percent of the population had ever tried illicit drugs, and American drug use was practically nonexistent in high schools. By 1978, almost 68 percent of high school students had tried marijuana and, more frighteningly, the average age of first use of illicit drugs had fallen to 12 and 13 years old.

These statistics confirmed many fears shared by parents of children approaching the age when drug abuse is common. In the initial phase of public drug awareness and parent interest groups, much lobbying was done against drug paraphernalia dealers who were selling to children and adolescents in local stores. In addition, parents established curfews and party rules so that their children would have specific guidelines to follow. These early efforts toward civilian drug suppression proved successful and the basic premise of preventative "parent power" was generally accepted. Augmenting the newfound emphasis on drug abuse awareness was First Lady Nancy Reagan's "Say No to Drugs" campaign in the mid-1980s. This prevention strategy has resulted in the expansion of drug prevention programs through the United States and many parts of the world.

Along with public concern regarding physical and mental drug dependence, the drug prevention component is now considered one of the more powerful allies in the war on drugs. It has been estimated that over 7,000 parents' organizations dedicated to fighting drug and alcohol abuse among young people now exist in small towns and suburbs around the country.

A prominent organization that helped pioneer the drug abuse prevention movement is PRIDE (The National Parents' Resource Institute for Drug Education, Inc.). This highly visible organization was organized in 1977 at Georgia State University to provide drug education and training for parents who wanted to fight back against the illicit drug culture and end the confusion about illicit drugs and their effects. Working with parents and teachers, PRIDE has effectively developed programs for parent education, collective behavioral guidelines and social alternatives for youth that are designed to reduce adolescent drug, alcohol and discipline problems.

PRIDE has evolved as a major force behind the organization of thousands of local parent/youth education programs. It informs and solicits assistance not only from parents but also from the news media, law enforcement agencies, the judicial system, health care professionals, churches and synagogues, the business community and the school system. Some of the services provided to interested neighborhood and community groups are:

1. Printed materials
2. Films, videotapes
3. A parent group coordinator to give organizational advice
4. A computerized network offering assistance to newcomers or established groups
5. A youth group coordinator who supplies printed material to children from kindergarten through high school
6. A community organization consultant to assist civic, business or religious groups in organizing anti-drug projects
7. A toll-free drug information phone bank providing up-to-date drug information

PRIDE has now expanded to include international anti-drug abuse programs in Canada, Panama, Pakistan, Belize, Finland, only to name a few. The basic philosophy of PRIDE and other similar groups is that prevention is the most powerful weapon against drug abuse and the best place to implement prevention is in the home.

According to a 1983 National Institute of Drug Abuse publication, entitled *Parents, Peers and Pot* by Doctor Marsha Manatt, some parents themselves may act as obstacles in the total prevention picture.

1. A parent's own sense of isolation and hurt
2. Parents as poor role models, using illicit drugs themselves
3. Parent apathy and non-involvement in anti-drug programs

Perhaps an initial stage of insecurity experienced by parents was due to conflicting information from professionals in medicine, social work and drug counseling. Many of these individuals spoke out against drug use in general, while others promoted "responsible use" of drugs and placed the blame for adolescent drug abuse on the parents.

Ultimately, parents become involved because of a gut-level instinct to protect the welfare of their children. Feelings of insecurity fade in light of public awareness and drug education programs offered to them. In addition, a sense of confidence and accomplishment is fostered in learning and identifying resources within local and community drug prevention organizations.

BIBLIOGRAPHY

1. Abadinsky, Howard. *Organized Crime.* 2nd ed. Chicago Nelson-Hall, Inc., 1985.
2. Albee, George W. "The Answer is Prevention." *Psychology Today,* February 1985: 60.
3. Castro, Janice. "Battling the Enemy Within." *Time,* 17 March 1986: 52.
4. Lyer, Pico. "Fighting the Cocaine Wars." *Time,* February 1985: 26.
5. Magnuson, Ed. "Hitting the Mafia." *Time,* 29 September 1986: 16.
6. Manatt, Marsha. *Parents, Peers and Pot.* U.S. Department of Human Services, National Institute on Drug Abuse, 1983.
7. Mann, Peggy. *Marijuana: The Myth Goes Up in Smoke.* Indianapolis, *The Saturday Evening Post,* 1980.
8. McAuliffe, William E., et al. *Psychoactive Drug Use Among Practicing Physicians and Medical Students.* Boston: Department of Behavioral Sciences. Harvard School of Public Health; *The New England Journal of Medicine,* September 25, 1986.
9. Morganthau, Tom, et al. "Crack and Crime." *Newsweek,* 16 June 1986: 16.
10. O'Brien, Robert and Cohen, Sidney, *The Encyclopedia of Drug Abuse.* New York, Facts On File, 1984.
11. President's Commission on Organized Crime. *America's Habit.* Report to the President, March 1986.
12. Schnoll, Sidney. *Getting Help; Treatments for Drug Abuse.* New York, Chelsea House Publisher, 1986.
13. Thomas, Evan. "America's Crusade." *Time,* 15 September 1986: 58.
14. Weil, Andrew. *Chocolate To Morphine.* Boston: Houghton-Mifflin Company, 1983.

INDEX